H. L. James'

RUGS AND POSTS

The Story of Navajo Weaving and Indian Trading

Schiffer Publishing Ltd

1469 Morstein Road, West Chester, Pennsylvania 19380

DEDICATION

For Joseph

For Ramona

For Stephanie

Monument Valley

Copyright © 1988 by H.L. James.
Library of Congress Catalog Number: 88-61473.

Printed in the United States of America.
ISBN: 0-88740-134-1
Published by Schiffer Publishing Ltd.
1469 Morstein Road, West Chester, Pennsylvania 19380

This book may be purchased from the publisher.
Please include $2.00 postage.
Try your bookstore first.

CONTENTS

About the cover . . .

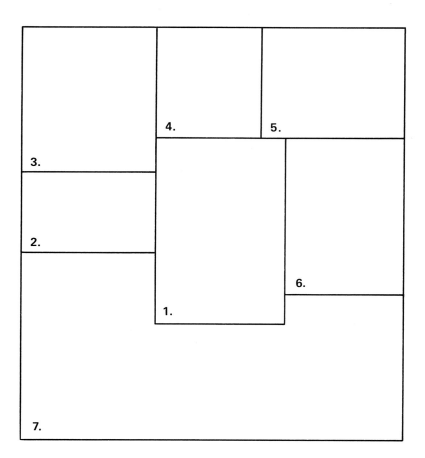

1. *Contemporary Ganado rug, 1987*
2. *Hubbell Trading Post, 1972.*
3. *Weavers, circa 1890.*
4. *Juan Lorenzo Hubbell, 1895.*
5. *Sunrise Springs Trading Post, 1935.*
   (Lt: Clarence A. Wheeler & Albert Hugh Lee).
6. *Rough Rock Trading Post, 1987.*
7. *Gathering at the sheep corral, Wide Ruins Trading Post, Christmas Day, 1941.*

Title page sketch, Shonto Trading Post, circa 1930.

by
Diane Nugent

ACKNOWLEDGMENTS

This type of book making, whether in the field or at a desk, is more exciting than laborous, both from the sorting of gathered research and from the people that are met along the way. There are many who assisted, but I am particularly indebted to two old-time Gallup friends, librarian Octavia Fellin, and Martin Link, editor of *The Indian Trader*. After several years of being away from the Southwest, these two enthusiastic providers of information were my principal contacts and, as always, were very cooperative and dependable. To Bruce Burnham of Sanders, Arizona, and Bill Malone at Hubbell Trading Post, for freely sharing their knowledge and providing insights on the state of Navajo weaving and Indian trading as it exists today. To Sallie Wagner of Santa Fe, and Fred Patton of Chinle, Arizona, for entrusting me with valuable photographs. And finally, to Shonto's Melissa Trolet, a little-known trader at a little-known place who, on that raw November day in 1987, offered a little-known writer a welcomed hand and a gracious respite—truly a spirit in keeping with Indian tradership of all times.

The art work in Chapter 2 was commissioned by Hallmark artist, Donald J. Mills of Evanston, Illinois. The title page sketch and layout/design consultations for the book are attributed to the talents of Diane Nugent of Butte, Montana.

March 15, 1988
Butte, MT

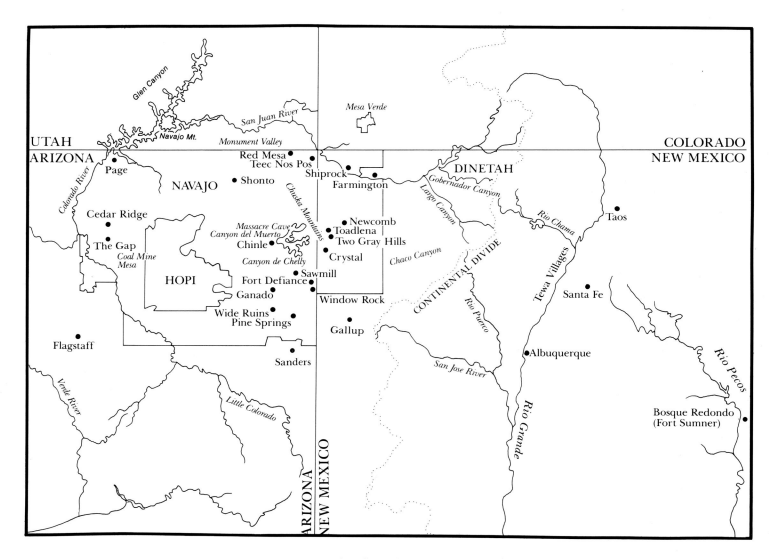

Dineth and environs.

Chapter 1

HISTORY

The People

They call themselves *Dine,* meaning simply "the people", and their homeland, *Dineth.* The word Navajo (Navaho) is of Tewa origin, which translates to "great planted fields." As determined from distributions of the Athapascan language, from which Navajo is derived, a nucleus of wandering clans crossed the Bering Strait about 3,000 years ago and moved gradually across what is presently southeastern Alaska and western Canada (Watson, 1973). Some anthropologists believe that a 700-year nomadic trek transpired that eventually led the Navajo and their kinsman, the Apache, into watersheds of the Chama and San Juan rivers some time around 1200-1400 A.D. Their exact route is uncertain, but logically the path of least resistance would lay along the eastern plains bordering the Rocky Mountains.

They had not made their presence felt by the year 1540, however, as chroniclers of Coronado's Expedition fail to mention them in their journals. The first known historical reference occurs in the *Relaciones* of Father Gerónimo Zárate de Salmerón, who wrote of their activities in the late 1500s. Fray Alonzo de Benavides also mentions them in 1630 as being good farmers.

Some time during the mid-1600s, their culture now well established and prosperous, there began an altering expansion with the Apaches severing ties and traveling south into desert environs to form their own *Dienth.* The early Spanish explorers referred to these people as the "Apache de Navahu". Perhaps because of drought, or friction with nearby Pueblo centers, the Navajo clans moved west and south to occupy a general area surrounding the sanctuary of Canyon de Chelly.

The wheels of Spanish occupation were set in motion by the advance of Coronado in 1540, followed four decades later by colonizers and the clergy under Juan de Oñate. The Spanish brought with them herds of churro-type sheep and goats—hence the origin of wool preparation and weaving in the Southwest.

The possession of the Rio Grande region under Spanish rule brought conflict. The Pueblo Indians became subserviant to the Europeans and suffered greatly by their dominance. This ultimately led to the Pueblo Revolt of 1680, whereby the Spanish were driven from the territory. Fearing reprisals, many Pueblo dwellers sought refuge and joined their neighbors to the west—hence the introduction of weaving skills to the Navajo.

Twelve years later, in 1692, Diego de Vargas reclaimed Nuevo Mexico, and a relatively peaceful period followed for most of the 18th century, broken occasionally by assults by Navajos to acquire livestock and goods. In turn, the Indians were becoming subjects of slave raids by the Spanish. In 1805, one such Spanish atrocity was the ruthless slaughter of over 100 elderly men, women and children huddled in a cave in a tributary of Canyon de Chelly. The place is now called Canyon del Muerto, Spanish for "canyon of the dead". Throughout the period the Navajos, now adept at their weaving skills, expanded their blanket trade network to include Plains Indians, as well as exchanges with the Spanish and the Pueblos.

Mexico gained its independence from Spain in 1821 and opened its boundaries to trade with the United States the following year with the warm reception of the first wagons over the Santa Fe Trail (James, 1966). This great commerce of the plains, which was to last in varying degrees until 1880, brought the Navajos a new source of supply in yarns, dyes and bolts of cloth in return for blankets that flowed into eager Anglo markets—a true cottage industry was now in place.

During Mexican rule (1821-1846), hostilities increased as slave raids were now initiated by both sides—the barter usually being for horses from neighboring tribes. This trafficking and plunder was, at the time of the American Acquisition in 1846, so prevalent that it ceased to be regarded as wrong. It was these unsettling attitudes that confronted the occupational Army Of The West, and as General Stephen Watts Kearney declared himself a "protector" instead of a conquerer, the resident population sensed perhaps a deliverance from their greatest menace—the marauding Indian. On September 18, 1846, Kearney dispatched three companies of Missouri Volunteers, under the command of Lt. Colonel Cosgreve Jackson, to the remote mission village of Seboyeta located sixty miles west of Albuquerque. No name was given to this frontier outpost and the garrison which was stationed there functioned mainly as a show of strength. The Seboyeta guard failed to impress the Indians; incursions and depredations continued to increase. In the weeks that followed, the situation worsened to the point where Kearney was continually besieged with delegations from communities all demanding protection from the Navajo menace. A changed course of action appeared necessary.

In 1846, a treaty approach was tried. Colonel Alexander W. Doniphan, representing General Kearney, met with Navajo chiefs on November 22nd at a noted rendezvous point in the northern foothills of the Zuni Mountains called Shash 'B Tow (Navajo for Bear Springs). In formal terms it was stated that the Navajos would swear allegiance with the Americans, and that all residents of the now-acquired territory would be administered by the United States government. Further it was stipulated that the Indians would cease all warlike activities against the residents of New Mexico. Also included were provisions for full restoration of all stolen property and livestock, and the release of all Mexican captives. The Indians made their mark upon a treaty paper; however, their outward show of friendship and good will was misleading. Their animosities toward the Mexicans were too deeply seated to be simply dissolved by the signing of a document.

The Doniphan Treaty proved to be a failure. Furthermore, the presence of a foreign military power in their homeland served only to incite the Indians. During the years 1847 to 1850, incursions and hostilities reached enormous proportions. Fort Marcy at Santa Fe became nothing more than a huge staging area for outfitting expeditions into Navajoland. More treaties were signed, more treaties were broken. Several peace negotiations failed even before the treaty expedition had returned to Santa Fe. It became an endless frustrating game to which a solution seemed impossible.

On July 19, 1851, a soldier of considerable experience, Colonel Edwin Vose Sumner, assumed command of the Ninth Military Department of New Mexico. He immediately undertook to revolutionize the whole system of frontier defense. He authorized a site for the erection of Fort Union (60 miles east of Santa Fe) to serve as departmental headquarters, replacing Fort Marcy. He withdrew the garrison from the Seboyeta outpost, and on September 18, 1851, issued general orders for the construction of still another post to be located along the east front of the Defiance Mountains. The site chosen was at a Navajo shrine called Tse Hot'

Sohih (Navajo meaning "meadows between the rocks"). The post was designed to house five companies and was appropriately named Fort Defiance.

Colonel Sumner, with his sometimes criticized reorganization, had the desired effect upon the Navajo—peace. To assure a lasting friendship he instituted commercial trade with the Indians. He directed the distribution of quartermaster stores to supplement the Tribe's needs during sterile winters. He provided technical services and agricultural aids. His assistance reached into Tribal government where he preached the advantages of affairs conducted in a democratic manner.

Fort Defiance remained the great fortress of peace for nearly eight years. Several violations of theft and murder did occur but the incidents were tactfully handled without provocation for war.

By the late 1850s the Indians became restless. This uneasiness grew from the reservation treaties of Meriwether (1855) and Bonneville (1858), in which the Navajos were geographically restricted within specified boundary lines. These limits were defined by the San Juan River on the north to the Zuni River on the south, at a point just east of Zuni Pueblo. The western boundary was placed along a line running south from the San Juan River (north of present Kayenta) to the confluence of Chevalon Creek and the Little Colorado River between present-day Holbrook and Winslow. The eastern boundary forbad all Indian claims east of Chaco Canyon. These treaties, although specifying their traditional lands, restricted their travel outside of the set boundaries. In short, the Navajos felt like prisoners in their own domain.

The strict conformity to reservation life, coupled with severe winters, forced many Navajos upon the plunder trail. A breach began to widen. Minor incidents became major incidents; plots were instigated. Finally, on the morning of April 30, 1860, the peace was broken. With the war-whoops of an estimated 1,000 warriors, Fort Defiance was attacked. The fort sustained itself for the entire day. Only until evening when darkness made it difficult to distinguish friend from foe did the Indians withdraw into the surrounding hills.

The brazen attack upon Fort Defiance threw New Mexico back into the grip of another Indian war. Additional troops of calvary reinforced the red-rock perimeters. Another post was established (August 31, 1860) on the grounds of the old Doniphan Treaty site at Bear Springs. It was named for the present Department Commander, Colonel Thomas Turner ("Little Lord") Fauntleroy. Throughout the remainder of 1860 and the early part of 1861 the United States Army became engaged in a full-scale Indian campaign, the likes of which the territory had never before witnessed.

In the Spring of 1861, the Military Department of New Mexico faced still another peril brought about by the secession of southern states, and the apparent Confederate plan to invade the desert Southwest. To

Fort Defiance, circa 1855.

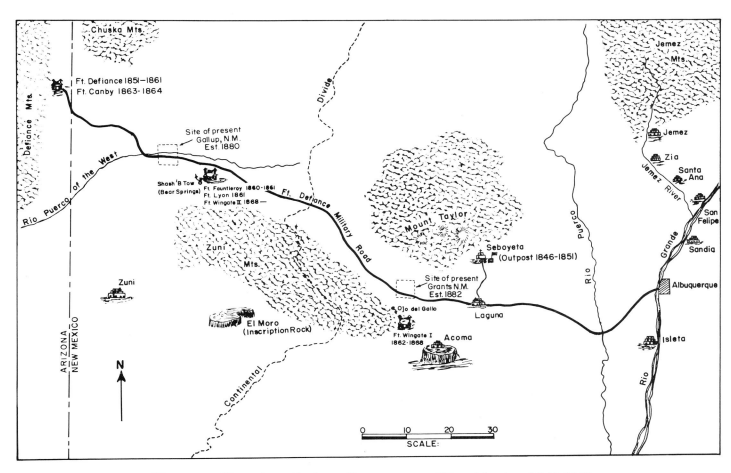

Western military installations. Department of New Mexico, 1846-1868.

meet this threatened invasion of the territory, the newly appointed Department Commander, Colonel Edward S. Canby, set the Indian problem aside and began concentrating his defenses closer to the Rio Grande. Fort Defiance was abandoned on April 25th, its garrison transferred to Fort Fauntleroy.

By the summer of 1861, the impending Confederate threat became a reality. On July 27th, Lt. Colonel John R. Baylor (C.S.A.), struck north from El Paso and captured Fort Fillmore (south of present-day Las Cruces). Baylor declared that all of New Mexico below Socorro to be Confederate territory, designating Mesilla as its capital.

On September 28, 1861, a general order of the U.S. Department of the Army changed the name of Fort Fauntleroy to Fort Lyon when Colonel Fauntleroy resigned his commission to join the Confederacy. The post's new name honored General Nathaniel Lyon who had been killed weeks earlier at the battle of Wilson Creek, Missouri.

Three months later, on December 10th, Fort Lyon was abandoned and the garrison was used to strengthen the forces at Fort Craig, below Socorro.

On February 14, 1862, the Texas Army (C.S.A), under the command of General Henry H. Sibley, who had replaced Colonel Baylor, began its tidal march up the Rio Grande. It defeated the Union forces at Fort Craig in the historic Battle of Valverde on February 21st. Continuing intact, General Sibley's army engulfed Albuquerque on March 2nd and Santa Fe on March 23rd. Their dreams of conquest were shattered, however, when they were badly defeated by Union troops, reinforced by Colorado Volunteers, at the Battle of Glorieta Pass, southeast of Santa Fe, on March 26th and 28th.

The Indians had taken full advantage of the military turmoil created by the Confederate invasion and their raids greatly increased during this period. In the summer of 1862, the new military commander for New Mexico, General James H. Carleton, turned his full attention to the Navajo. His plans for the complete submission of the Tribe called for a "roundup" and placing them on a supervised military reservation; the philosophy being, "it is cheaper to feed them then to fight them". His "Indian policy" also included the authorization of a new post to be built on the eastern slopes of the Zuni Mountains to serve as staging area for his plan. General Carleton named the new post Fort Wingate to honor Captain Benjamin A. Wingate, an infantry officer who had served at Fort Lyon, and who had died of wounds during heroic conduct in the Battle of Valverde (James, 1967).

The site chosen for the fort was at Ojo del Gallo (Spanish for Chicken Spring) near the present-day city of Grants, New Mexico. Construction began on September 30, 1862. The actual erection of permanent buildings was a slow process, as materials were salvaged and hauled by wagon from old Fort Lyon 45 miles to the west. The fort was formally commissioned on October 22, 1862.

On November 9, 1862, Carleton notified the War Department of the establishment of still another post, to be named Fort Sumner in honor of the old campaigner of the 1850s, Edwin Vose Sumner. The fort was located 165 miles southeast of Santa Fe at a point on the east side of the Rio Pecos known as Bosque Redondo (Spanish for Round Grove). This post would supervise Carleton's internment camp of the Navajos.

By the spring of 1863, Fort Wingate was beginning to take shape. Four companies of the Fourth New Mexico Mounted Rifles and one company of California Volunteers, under the command of Lt. Colonel Jose Francisco Chavez, had taken up quarters. In addition to these troops the garrison was further strengthened by Colonel Christopher "Kit" Carson's E, F and H companies of the First New Mexico Volunteers—a force of 736 men (Fontana, 1988).

Carleton was now ready to take the field against the Navajo. In his first movement, on July 28, 1863, he directed Carson to set up a base of operation at the ruins of old Fort Defiance (renamed Fort Canby). He then sent word to all chiefs that total war was to commence, and that any Navajo not wishing to engage in these hostilities could surrender at either Fort Wingate or Fort Canby. Some Indians, observing the strength building of the "blue coats", and the proclamation of a vigorous war, began surrendering in small groups. By fall the count was 180 tribesmen, a number quite short of Carleton's idea of total supression.

In mid-October 1863, Carleton released the full fury of his "Indian policy". He undertook a scorched-earth campaign the likes of which the Indians had never imagined. Carson's troops pursued them night and day, week after week, over mesas, mountains, and deserts, and through drifts of winter snows. The military pursuit included the needless destruction of planting fields, grain storages, the burning of hogans and orchards, and the wanton slaughter of sheep and cattle. By the end of 1863, the Navajos found themselves in a desperate state. To worsen matters they lay in the grip of a severe winter faced with complete extermination, not only by the saber but from exposure and hunger. On January 12, 1864, Carson delivered the final blow by attacking their only remaining stronghold—Canyon de Chelly. There, huddled together, demoralized, too weak to resist, the once proud lords of the canyonlands submitted to the will of the white man.

On March 4, 1864, more than two thousand Navajos filed out of Fort Canby and began the infamous trek to Fort Sumner that is known in history today as the "Long Walk", a 350-mile journey to the Rio Pecos. The route soon displayed a stream of ragged humanity that continued throughout 1864. The pathway was marked by the remains of many Indians who crawled to the wayside to die a lingering death through dysentery and exposure.

Carleton had envisioned his 40-square-mile reservation to be a self-supporting agricultural system, but the 6,000 acres set aside for tilling were found to be impregnated with alkali, and as a consequence the yield of crops was low. By the beginning of 1865, the population had grown in excess of 9,000, which included some 400 renegade Apaches transferred from Fort Stanton. The large population, coupled with the first years crop failure, began to tax the army's quartermaster in its quest for food.

From the beginning, the troubles at Bosque Redondo were compounded by dissention and natural disorders. Conflicts broke out between Navajos and Apaches, Indian agents and the military, and between civil authorities and the military. Inadequate food and clothing was a prime cause of disorder. The confined were undernourished and plagued by disease. The brackish water from the river resulted in mass dysentery. Desertions and "runaways" were frequent. Added to this, prisoners in unprotected sectors became the targets of bands of Comanches and Kiowas who roamed the vast Llano Estacado to the east.

Bosque Redondo became nothing more than a huge concentration camp without regard to the preservation of human life. It soon fell under attack by civic leaders of the territory who demanded a complete investigation of conditions. The tremendous expenditure necessary

to maintain the compound also was questioned and came under attack. Finally, the shameful disgrace of the encampment reflected on the people of the Territory and aroused political feelings to the point where candidates and parties were labeled either "pro-Bosque" or "anti-Bosque". Editorials were demanding the resignation of General Carleton.

The plight of the Navajos began attracting national attention that could no longer be ignored. On March 3, 1865, a Joint Special Committee composed of members of both houses of Congress was appointed to investigate conditions along the Rio Pecos. The committee, headed by chairman James R. Doolittle of Wisconsin, personally inspected Bosque Redondo during the month of July. Their findings resulted in a report which recommended that the care of the Indians be transferred from military control to one of civil authority, namely, the Department of the Interior.

Charges and countercharges were hurled in both directions over the report. In early 1866, the Territorial Assembly in Santa Fe joined the controversy by publicly condemning Carleton's "Indian policy". They adopted a resolution which was personally forwarded to President Andrew Johnson, urging the removal of the departmental commander.

After much debate, the government slowly began to grind out a solution. Finally, on September 19, 1866, the first steps were taken. General James H. Carleton was relieved of his position and replaced by General G.W. Getty. On December 31st the control of the

Bosque Redondo, 1866.

Navajos under guard at the internment camp. Late Classic Period shoulder wraps designed with broad stripes and bands are much in evidence.

Indians was assigned to a Commissioner of Indian Affairs under the Department of Interior. The military was instructed to give assistance in Indian problems only when requested by the Commissioner.

The Secretary of Interior and the Commissioner of Indian Affairs, with the authority delegated by Congress, entertained the proposition of returning the Navajos to their homeland. The Interior Department appointed a committee to survey the resources of their original reservation in hopes of relocating them back on their native soil. When all reports were favorably accepted, a Peace Commission, headed by Lt. General William Tecumseh Sherman, was selected to negotiate a treaty. Sherman arrived at Fort Sumner on May 28, 1867. Three days later a treaty was drafted and accepted by the dejected Indians. They were now allowed to reverse the "Long Walk," and at sunrise, on the morning of June 18, 1868, a column of Indians which reportedly stretched for 10 miles, began the return to their beloved redrocks and their ravaged homeland.[1]

The Navajos called their time at Bosque Redondo, *Nabondzod*, "the fearing time" (Utley and Washburn, 1977). If that period on the Rio Pecos seemed dreadful, what lay ahead during the early days of resettlement was not much better. As specified by the treaty, the Indians were to receive food, clothing, tools and supplies, and education for their children for a period of ten years. In the fall of 1869, more than 9,000 Navajos gathered at Fort Defiance for a sheep distribution allotment that consisted of two animals for every man, woman and child (Koenig and Koeing, 1986). The economic and social dependency of the Fort Defiance "ration days", and government reliance that has prevailed into the modern era, have been inextricably linked ever since.

Fort Defiance ration days, circa 1870.

The Traders

The involvement of the federal government to regulate commerce with Indian tribes dates back to April 18, 1796, when President George Washington signed a bill to establish "trading houses" to serve various southern and western Indian nations. This was followed on June 30, 1835, by an Act of Congress to Regulate Trade and Intercourse with Indian Tribes. [With the Acquisition of 1846, this Act was later revised to include tribes of the Southwest.]

The early Indian traders were a rugged phenom and functioned in an independent lifestyle that required endurance, perserverence and a dash of ingenuity; a "wooley lot", if you will, with a keen sense for the slightest margin of profit. They spawned from that breed of French trappers in the southern Rockies to Comancheros who bartered their questionable inventories from the packs of wandering caravans on the Great Plains.

The first Navajo trader who operated from a fixed location was George A. Richardson, who was licensed on October 26, 1865, to administer the store at Bosque Redondo. Later, other licenses were issued at the camp to Joseph A. LaRue, Oscar M. Brown and W.W. Martin.[2]

The "true" trading post evolved when the Navajos were released to the guardianship of the Bureau of Indian Affairs at Fort Defiance. Authorized by Congress, the Commissioner now had the sole power to license and appoint traders. The Fort Defiance traders were: Lehman Spiegelberg of Santa Fe, who was licensed on August 28, 1868, Cole F. Ludlove of Valencia County, New Mexico (October 1868), and John Ayres of Abuquiu, New Mexico (1870), followed by his brother, Lionel, in 1872.

As the Indians slowly dessimentated throughout the remote recesses of their homeland, so did the trading post. As these "general stores" sprang up, a unique entrepreneural institution began to emerge—headed by a middleman who served two worlds of exchange; flour, coffee, canned goods, tools and clothing in return for woven products, wool, sheep, hides, and in good years, piñon nuts.[3]

Every person who traded on the Navajo Reservation did so with government approval—revokable at any time. The rules were strict, although not always enforceable. A bond of $10,000 was required up front and issued only to U.S. citizens who could demonstrate exceptional character and satisfactory references. The trader was responsible for the conduct of his employees. They were also held accountable for price lists and monthly invoices, which were audited by the Bureau. Articles of merchandise were fixed by said office and the allowable return of profit on any item could not exceed 25 percent of the cost of the goods, plus freight (Commissioner of Indian Affairs Annual Report, 1886). The sale of ammunition, firearms and alcoholic beverages were definitely prohibited, however, off-reservation outlets and nearby towns were available for such purchases.

The prequisites for successful trading usually included a favored location (with water), such as at a point where established travel routes existed, or in an area where several clans might settle. This would ensure a population base upon which to build a reliable clientele. Learning the Navajo language (in a hurry) was a must; establishing some early rapport with headsmen was tactful; a willingness to extend reasonable credit (pawn) showed business sense; and of course, marrying a "local girl" couldn't hurt—several did. If a new trader was resourceful, he would soon begin working with area weavers by suggesting certain dyes and designs, and in return paying a top price for the best products.[4]

The early facilities were crude—nothing more than tents or adobe (mud) huts. Since land ownership was prohibited, most traders never considered equity or home improvements a very high priority, therefore, the posts were usually of modest means and costs, if not primitive in some cases.[5]

If the site was in or near a mountain locale, the construction was of logs; in desert valleys it was usually of sandstone slabs cemented with mud. The store was often small with living quarters in the back. Space was limited, particularly when the place also served as a social center for the exchange of news. The atmosphere of the trading post, with its seemingly endless array of colorfully labeled goods and modern implements, was awesome to the Navajo and might be compared in kind to what a major shopping mall would be to the present-day urbanite. The front door opened into a sort of compound called a "bullpen"—a corral-type enclosure bounded by high counters on three sides. A pot-bellied stove usually occupied the center floor plan with wooden benches outlining the perimeter. NcNitt (1962, p. 75) best describes the scene:

Shelves behind the high counters, therefore, were loaded to ceiling level: groceries on this side, dry goods on that side. Still there was not enough room to display everything, and so the roof beams dripped merchandise as a cave roof collects stalactites. From hooks and nails dangled Dutch ovens and frying pans of dull black iron, glinting oil lanterns, and hardware—tin pots and kettles and washtubs—coils of yellow rope, bridles, saddles, and tanned deer hides or skins of mountain lions. The smell of the post always was the same, desert or mountain: a concentrated essence of very dry dust, of sweet tanned leather and sour sweat and oil and metal, an abrasive lining of spit, tobacco smoke, and kerosene, and sometimes, for charity's sake, a whiff of sagebrush carried through the chinks and cracks of walls and roof.

Arbuckles Coffee—the stable of common ground. Perhaps no other single product confirmed more deals, established friendships, or bonded two races of people than "Hosteen Cohay." A long favorite of the Navajo, the Ariosa brew played an important role in reservation life. The wooden shipping crates provided materials for infant cradle boards, repair of post walls, gates and corrals, use in store counters and shelving, and the building of sheds, privies and outbuildings. Even the one-pound paper packaging was imprinted with various prize signatures, which could be redeemed for a penny or a stick of candy.

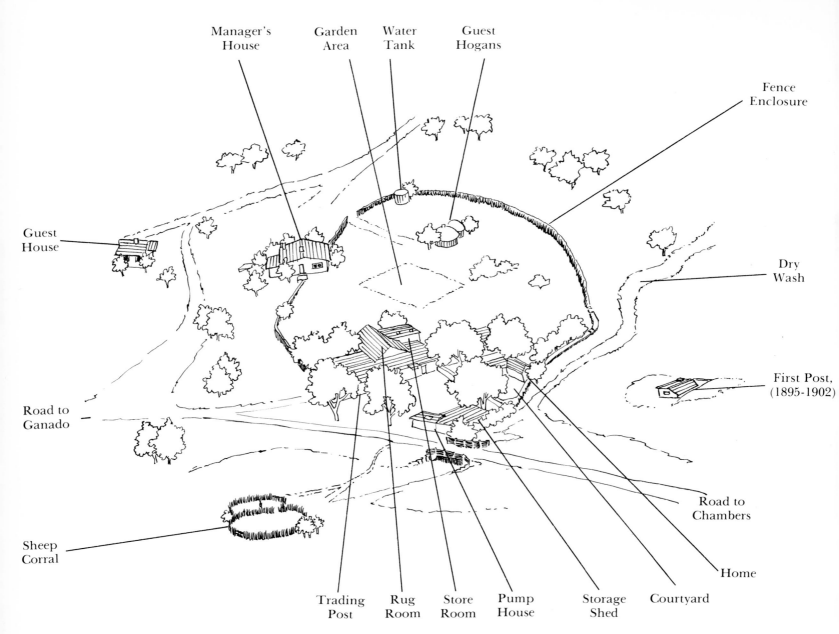

Manager's House   Garden Area   Water Tank   Guest Hogans

Fence Enclosure

Guest House

Dry Wash

First Post, (1895-1902)

Road to Ganado

Road to Chambers

Sheep Corral

Home

Trading Post   Rug Room   Store Room   Pump House   Storage Shed   Courtyard

Anatomy of a trading post—Wide Ruins, circa 1940.

If business prospered and the trader felt acceptance in his chosen role some expansion was in order, and soon the place would take on the appearance of a small settlement. In time, a warehouse, barn, corrals and various out buildings were added. At some places, a guest hogan was constructed nearby.[6]

Lonliness was one major obstacle to cope with, particularly if a post was located in a remote area. Traders who were single, without any family or hired help, could find themselves in a desperate state of solitude at times. More often it was in the winter when deep snows inhibited even horse traffic, causing days, even weeks to pass without contact with another person. Some traders became "spooked" with this aspect of the business and several left the reservation for more personable endeavors.

With the advent of tourism in the early part of the 20th century, the trader found a new source of revenue—the sightseeing Anglo. To serve these dauntless travelers, the trading post also became a retail outlet for rugs, as well as providing food, supplies, and another duty to tend to—pumping gas. With all variables now in place, these remote havens functioned as an integral component of consumer economy on the reservation and became indispensible emporiums for goods and services.

The trader became the main link between the Anglo world and the remote civilization of the reservation Indian. Other than the daily responsibilities of store keeping, he acted as their spokesman beyond the boundaries of their world. Displaying compassion and sensitivity, he lent an understanding ear and served as their benefactor, counselor and protector. He advised in medical and legal matters, mediated disputes, assisted in chores, help bury their dead, marketed their goods, and in the process became loved and respected by all that he attended. As trust was garnered, he became highly influencial in his trade area.

In 1868, the initial three licenses that were granted to commence trade with the Navajos was doubled by 1877.

At the turn of the century there were 36, and in 1943, the heyday of the Navajo trader, there were 95 government-licensed posts on the reservation, with an additional 50 or more operating outside the boundaries (Ledger of Licensed Indian Traders, U.S. National Archives, Washington, D.C., n.d.). It has been declining in number ever since.

Following World War II, attitudes changed on the reservation. Six thousand returning Navajo veterans, now armed with knowledge of other people, other lands and other ways, had increased their awareness of broader values—employment, education and a desire to enter the mainstream of the outside world. With this changing philosophy, the *naalyé hé báhoogan* (the trading post), no longer became the center of their cultural existence and, although continuing as a supplier of goods and a center for marketing, its role as a dominant societal influence was beginning to diminish.

New trends continue to sweep the reservation, and in the modern era it is forcing the old-time trader into the twilight of his time. With these trends comes the inevitable quote of "progress". Where wagon ruts and sheep trails once wandered, there are now seemingly endless stretches of asphalt highways. When once it took days to haul trade goods from the railroad, they are now delivered in hours—in refrigerated carriers, no less. The traditional values of the past are now being replaced by modern conveniences. A paradox, if you will, of weighing the values of an existence in a primitive land, but exercising the choice of purchasing assorted frozen dinners and a good selection of VCR movies.

Since 1980, over half of the active trading posts operating at that time have either closed, burned, lost leases, or have been purchased by a convenience store chain. Trade centers such as Chinle, the very core of Navajo tradition, no longer supports a true trader. Place names synonymous with rug styles like Wide Ruins and Burnt Water, no longer exist. Others are marked for change and perhaps before the end of this century, the last trader will become inundated beneath the "wave of progress", thus ending a 130-year era of remarkable coexistence with a red brethren in a red land.

Epilogue
"The day is not too far off when the [Tribal] council will allow all sorts of businesses to operate on the reservation, and this will mark the end of the old Indian trader".

Roman Hubbel, 1948
Gallup *Independent*

The Craft

Much has been written on the history of Navajo weaving. It is generally agreed that the events of the craft are categorized into six periods of development: Classic Period (1700-1850), Late Classic Period (1850-1863), Transition Period (1868-1890), Rug Period (1890-1930), Revival Period (1930-1940) and the Regional Style Period (1940-present).

Classic Period (1700-1850)

The Navajos learned the art of weaving on upright looms (as opposed to Hispanic horizontal looms) from

Tourists - Bless Them!

Pueblo Indians who fled into Navajo sanctuaries following the revolt of 1680, although some cotton weaving may have been gleaned from them somewhat earlier in that century.[7] Crude clothing was the main objective—dresses, shirts and breech cloths, shoulder blankets, leggings, belts, hair cords and ponchos.

The earliest surviving examples from Massacre Cave (1805) show that patterns were simple, primarily in narrow stripes and bands. Colors were mostly the natural wool tones of white, gray, brown, tan and black. Some vegetal dying was used in ranges of rust, yellow and green. Indigo blue was introduced early by the Spanish and became widely used throughout the period.

Some trade in blankets with the Spanish began on a small scale in the 1700s, as well as with other Pueblo neighbors. During the latter part of the period, Spanish enslavement of some Navajos resulted in the first definitive style piece, the so-called "slave blanket". In the 1800s, woven Mexican-Saltillo serapes were finding their way into markets in the upper Rio Grande region. These products would soon influence and inspire Navajo weavers into design adaptations, particularly the diamond and broad, wavy band motifs.

Late Classic Period (1850-1863)

In the 150 years or so after they began weaving, the Navajo far surpassed their Pueblo teachers as weavers and suppliers of blankets for the Spanish, other Indian tribes, and by 1850, to American soldiers and settlers; the period brought the weavers increasing economic success. The popular shoulder wrap for men, distinctively patterned in broad black, blue (indigo) and white horizontal bands, was termed the Chief Blanket.[8] This widely sought after fabric was later modified to encorporate red bayeta threads with design alterations of diamonds, boxes, crosses and stripes. The blanket was very popular among other Indian tribes and U.S. military leaders.

The serape and the poncho serape were also major period pieces. The latter woven longer than wide, and with a slit for the head, was draped over the wearer's body to form a front and back. Most serapes were fashioned in Mexican-Saltillo designs of serrated diamonds and broad wavy bands. Woven on horizontal looms, the Mexican pieces were usually constructed in half panels, and then sewn together to fashion the full fabric.

Experimentation in design and pattern highlighted the Late Classic Period, along with a greater technical excellence in spinning and weaving. Unable to produce brilliant red, the Navajo traded for bolts of English manufactured baize (a wool cloth called bayeta in Spanish).[9] The weavers unraveled the red fabric, respun the threads and used them in combinations with native wool. American flannel, when available, was similarly used. Additional imports into the Southwest, through Spain, Mexico and United States frontier routes, were the pre-aniline, three-ply European yarns, called

Saxony. The combination of bayeta red and indigo blue, used with the distinctive sheens of Saxony, yielded highly marketable items. With new colors came inventiveness in design, such as terraced motifs, zigzags, diamonds and outlined crosses.

By the early 1860s the golden age of weaving had arrived, but at its seemingly grandest hour, the textile revolution of the period tragically collapsed with the fall and imprisonment of the Navajo people.

Deprived of natural wool while in exile, weavers turned to machine-made yarn supplied by their captors and continued to make blankets for sale.

Transition Period (1868-1890)

With their pacification, the Navajos were allowed to return to their beloved redrocks. Now faced with the task of rebuilding their sheep flocks and wool supply, the freed weavers, becoming familiar with commercial yarn, slowly began to embark on a wild extravaganza of color. Bayeta and Saxony wools of the Late Classic Period were replaced in the early 1870s by a newly introduced yarn called Germantown. This was a coarse, four-ply and three-ply, aniline-dyed yarn, much of it manufactured in western Pennsylvania. At the height of Germantown use (1890) came a period of decline; design carelessness and gaudy color balances became the rule.[10] The commercial aspects of the craft became misdirected and drifted into confusion.

Sharing the period of resettlement with the Navajo was a new breed of man, the Indian trader, a unique type of individual who bridged the great gap between the red and white races. By the late 1870s, government-licensed traders were spreading across the reservation, setting up remote outposts of goods and personally concerning themselves with the promotion of weaving. The imagination of the trader brought new stimulus to the craft. Goods sold by traders introduced the weavers to a new field of visual designs—the alphabet, patterns on supply sacks, pictures and catalogs.

As the 20th century approached, the weaving industry slowly regained its balance. There were two main reasons for this change: (1) the trader and the development of regional styles of weaving and (2) the transition from blanket to rug. Rugs were created when weavers stopped making blankets for themselves, turning instead to another trader-provided item, the machine-made Pendleton blanket, as wearing apparel. The result was a new-found market for heavier and larger weaves, supplying the white man with floor coverings. Commercial Germantown yarns generally lost favor with traders, and weavers turned again to using handspun wool.

Rug Period (1890-1930)

Already in use by the 1880s, commercial dyes (now available in individual color packets) were gaining favor on the reservation, and the new colors gave greater intensity to the fine textiles that were being produced.[11] New styles were experimented with, one of the most significant being the bordered rug. The

Chief Blanket, circa 1865.

Germantown "Eyedazzler," circa 1878.

Ganado, circa 1891.

Cayatanito, 1874.

Bayeta, circa 1840.

framed format was encouraged by traders for its appeal to eastern clientele. By 1920, few rugs left the loom without some form of outside band to enclose the pattern.[12]

By the early 1900s came the greatest rug market the industry had yet known, and production was soon pressed to keep up with demand. The greatest stimuli was an increasing awareness of the Native American culture. Informational outgrowths from archaeological expeditions, Indian fairs, inter-tribal ceremonials, curio outlets, art, photography and publications all benefited the Navajo marketplace.

With improved rail transportation and back roads, there appeared a new singular force—"the tourist", an intripid soul with laced-up boots, camera in hand, and money for the purchase of crafts. Fulfilling dreams of exploration in aboriginal America, they came in droves, many rocking along on a train whose very name stirred excitement—"The Santa Fe Chief". They caravaned in canvas-topped Buicks and touring Packards—all in search of wonderous places, and in the process, purchased thousands of Navajo rugs as evidence of their adventure.

The Fred Harvey Company, under the aegis of the Santa Fe Railroad, developed a popular sight-seeing concession called *Indian Detours*. From a headquarters at the La Fonda Hotel in Santa Fe, Hunter Clarkston managed a personalized service which featured "Harveycars" (complete with picnic hampers), drivers dressed in Western outfits and tour hostesses adorned in velveteen blouses and turquoise jewelry. During this era, and extending well into the 1950s, these excursions crisscrossed the multi-colored deserts from Canyon de Chelly to the Grand Canyon and contributed significantly to the economy of the reservation.

Two traders of the period, Juan Lorenzo Hubbell of Ganado, Arizona, and John B. Moore of Crystal, New Mexico, greatly influenced the growth of the craft. Hubbell demanded quality, discouraging inferior dyes and loose-woven fabrics. He encouraged a return to

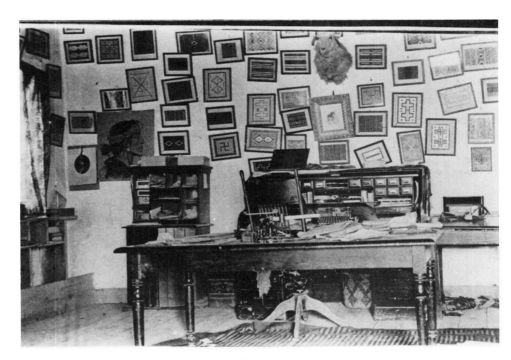

Hubbell's office showing wall hangings of commissioned art work of rug designs.

Hubbell Trading Post, 1890. Obviously posed, this scene illustrates the prolific rug market which existed near the turn of the century. Hubbell (foreground) apparently chose to exhibit and publicize his inventory of Chief Blanket-type rugs, indicating its enduring popularity. He is seated upon a rather large example—facing no doubt its creator. Another Chief-designed fabric is "clotheslined" on the left, while three more can be identified hanging from the post walls in the background. Note the extremely large Ganado-style rug draped on the fence to the right; the size trait was a Hubbell specialty. This rug is now in collection at The Museum of Northern Arizona in Flagstaff.

"Harveycar" and Indian Detour guests in New Mexico, circa 1929.

Late Classic Period designs of bold crosses, stripes and diamonds which were set against a brilliant red, aniline-dyed background that was bordered in black. He commissioned artists E.A. Burbank, Bertha A. Little, and others to paint rug patterns in oil and watercolor, and these samples were hung in his post for weavers to copy. Hubbell also urged the weaving of heavier products—durable pieces in larger sizes to be used as area rugs in the home. In return, he promised "his" weavers higher sales in a greater market. The Fred Harvey Company stocked hundreds of the famed "Ganado reds" in their tourist outlets along the Santa Fe Railroad, and the rug became famous.[13]

John B. Moore was also a disciple of craftsmanship. He had weavers bring in raw wool which he then sent to eastern mills for machine cleaning.[14] When returned, the processed wool could be spun and woven more evenly. The technical quality of Moore-based rugs met with immediate success. Like Hubbell, he published mail-order catalogs outlining grades of wool, classes of rugs, and prices. These now out-of-print and rare booklets were illustrated with photographs of weavers at work, and contained the first color plates of Navajo rugs. His distinctive styles included a bordered rug with the natural wool tones of black, brown and white coupled with carded blends of gray, tan and beige, and used in combinations with commercial dyes of red and blue. Moore's greatest contribution was perhaps the designs that he originated. In the years to come, his basic patterns would give rise to a popular regional style rug called the *Two Gray Hills.*

Beginning in 1910, Navajo weaving started a descent into its second depression. During this time the federal government, hoping to improve meat capacities of the tribe, introduced large flocks of French Rambouillet sheep to the reservation. The new animal was a good producer, both in mutton and fleece, but for weaving purposes it was a disaster. The new wool was short and oily, difficult to clean, card, spin and weave. Many rugs coming off the loom were heavy and coarse textured. The white patterns showed dirty gray casts, and when dyed with bright colors, the wool reflected a loss of brilliance. Designs became stereotyped, causing prices and demand to fall drastically in some areas. To stimulate production, traders began buying rugs by the pound (called "pound rugs"). Weavers responded and began to weave the wool without eliminating grease and dirt, thus increasing its weight. Some weavers went to such extremes as to saturate their rugs with "rubbed-in" dirt. Penalties were imposed for this practice, but it could not be controlled. By the late 1920s, a gloom of lost initiative had settled over some weaving areas on the reservation.

Extra fine and perfectly cleaned, per piece, $10.00 to $50.00 each, according to size and quality.

I have no saddle blankets nor common ones to quote.

Any of the grade will be shipped on approval with the understanding that the customer assumes all transportation costs both ways in case of return; and that no deductions on this account be allowed from invoice price in case of acceptance. We will ship, prepay, allow deductions from invoice price, on the extra fine ones of this grade, priced per piece, just the same as on the "ER-20" class, but only on these, of this "T-XX" class.

A FEW HINTS FOR THE CUSTOMER IN ORDERING

You always get the best value for your money in the higher priced rugs. You will be, and must be, pleased in these, and are assured against the possibility of buying and paying for a thing not satisfactory, by the return privilege allowed on all fine rugs.

You get just the size, the colors, and the pattern wanted, if you order from the "ER-20" class. If it is not in stock when your order comes, and you are willing to allow us a reasonable time in which to have it done, we will have it made for you especially. In this way you get something exclusive without the least danger of any other ever having something just like it.

Do not order the best quality and stipulate the lowest price. We wish in all cases to give the best possible value for the money and know that we do it, but I nor no other can sell our best goods for our lowest prices.

(Continued on page 25)

By permission Sim. Schwemberger.

NAVAJO RUG IN THE MAKING—The finished job
(Do you recognize the XXIV pattern?)

A sample page from the 1911 Moore catalog. John B. Moore is shown with one of "his" weavers illustrating a "top-of-the-line, ER-20 grade rug." Note the broad border, latch hook elements, and central cross patterns—all characteristically Moore favorites, which may have been Mediterranean inspired.

Revival Period (1930-1940)

As is generally the case in most individual endeavors, a period of deterioration is usually followed by one of distinction. Some dedicated person or persons takes on the task for reversing the tide and thus brings forth a new level transcending all previous efforts.

Several persons were responsible for the craft's second rejuvenation. Most notable were Nija and Leon H. McSparron of Chinle, Arizona. By the early 1930s, in association with a Navajo benefactress named Mary C. Wheelright, they had undertook a program to encourage weavers of that district to experiment with the old vegetal-dye methods that were used prior to introduction of commercial colorants (1878). The Chinle weavers ultimately developed pastel hues of browns, golds and greens in Classic Period patterns of simple stripes and bands set on a borderless fabric—thus was conceived the *Chinle* regional style.

Encouraged by the restoration of soft vegetal-dye tones, but desiring a more varied color palate, Miss Wheelright questioned the feasibility of creating such colors from commercial dyes. Subsequently, tests were initiated with the DuPont Chemical Company. The result was a series of manufactured dyes in a highly concentrated form, using 28 percent acetic acid as a mordant to be mixed with a desired colorant. In 1932, the dyes were introduced on the reservation. The solutions resulted in beautifully colored yarns, and weavers were pleased by the flexibility of tones that could be achieved. In the months that followed, the Diamond Dye Company of Burlington, Vermont, produced an improved series called *Old Navaho*. This product combined in one package the mordant with the colorant, thus relieving the weaver of the hazardous procedures of acid mixings. Today, the *Chinle* regional style rug reflects both the vegetal and commercial dye experiments of the Revival Period.

Further experimentation with native plant dyes was undertaken in the late 1930s by Bill and Sallie Lippincott of Wide Ruins Trading Post. They encouraged area weavers in the selection of subtle colors. Their labors met with excellent results, giving rise to a distinctive, well-woven product called the *Wide Ruins*, which today denotes an all-vegetal dyed rug.

The success of vegetal dyes did not end with the field tests at Chinle and Wide Ruins, but was carried on in laboratory experiments at Fort Wingate Vocational High School east of Gallup, New Mexico. Here two women, Nonabah G. Bryan and Stella Young, conducted six years of research on native plants. A combination resulting in 84 shades of color dyes. Findings of their study were published in 1940 under the title, *Navajo Native Dyes, Their Preparation and Use*, by the U.S. Department of The Interior. The recipe, instruction-type manual was widely circulated both on and off the reservation, and for those weavers who desired to work with vegetal-dye methods, the

Commissioner Collier and unidentified Navajo elder, 1933.

step-by-step procedures became an invaluable aid. In recent years, over 240 color tones have been achieved from native plant dyes, and the combinations from them are innumerable. This research and its application represents one of the greatest contributions to Navajo weaving. The improved esthetic quality of the vegetal-dye products, in the eyes of the white man, has in all probability extended the life of the craft.

Several other significant events occurred before the close of the Revival Period. First, overgrazing on range lands by rapidly increasing sheep flocks had first been identified as early as 1880. Government requested (voluntary) stock reductions had been unsuccessful and by 1920 a struggle began to emerge between what federal officials perceived to be prudent land management and what the Navajo culture held to be sacred gifts—their animals. In a 1933 decision, Commissioner John Collier implemented a hasty, poorly planned Stock Reduction Program which included law-enforced reductions of all flocks and herds on the reservation, regardless of size and ownership. To decree that all animals were to be lessened equally was terribly inequitable, as it had little effect on large operations, while small herders were virtually wiped out. Understandably, chaos developed out of the program with some areas actually experiencing wasteful slaughter of animals to meet mandatory numbers. The economic impact in wool, mutton, hide and rug losses was significant for a time, not to mention imposing poverty levels on some family units in declining livelihoods. Fortunately, the program was reevaluated and the reservation was divided into grazing districts requiring permits in relation to animal/pasturage ratios. The emotional pain of the Stock Reduction Program remains with the Navajo to this day, and is second only to the "Long Walk" in its trauma.

On a more positive side, was establishment of the Navajo Sheep Breeding Laboratory at Fort Wingate in 1934. Directed by the U.S. Department of Agriculture, programs were initiated to improve the Rambouillet strain, mainly through selective breeding with existing flocks. The success of the project provided a balance between high mutton yield and finer grades of fleece. And lastly, came the founding of the Navajo Arts and Crafts Guild in 1941. This Window Rock-based organization provided quality controls and protection for the weaver, as well as assistance in procurement of good weaving materials and fair market outlets.

Regional Style Period (1940-Present)

As previously outlined, four areas were beginning to emerge as style centers in preceding periods—the Moore-*Crystal* and Hubbell—*Ganado* during the Rug Period (1890-1920), and the McSparron—*Chinle* and Lippincott—*Wide Ruins* in the Revival Period (1920-1940). Early in the development of the Regional Style Period, weavers in other areas sought to create new designs, ideas, and arrangements of patterns and colors that would be commercially attractive. Those rugs whose history began with imaginative traders became the standard bearers of the period. Other areas at one time or another that were considered style centers, but failing to develop distinction through trader encouragement and guidance, or through merging of characteristics with stronger centers, soon lost their identities.

By the 1950s there were six additional style-type rugs that were recognized and associated with certain geographic locations on the reservation: *Shiprock, Teec Nos Pos, Lukachukai, Two Gray Hills,* the "new" *Crystal,* and the area designated as Western Reservation. [Some writers recognize different separations in regional style weaving centers, *see correlation chart, p. 30-31.*] Each of these regional types is different, characterized by its own distinctive style, color, dye and design that can be identified at a glance as to its weaving center. In succeeding years an element of pride developed in these centers to emphasize the individualism of style.[15]

It is interesting to note that while the regional style rug is the most publicized textile in Navajoland at the present time, it accounts for only about 25 percent of total rug production. There is no law governing regional style weaving. Some weavers, regardless of their reservation home, may prefer the vegetal dyes and designs of a *Crystal* while residing near Ganado. A few are classed as combination weavers. These rare artists, who usually live in the vicinity of two rug regions, can produce two styles of design of equal excellence. Not all weavers are geared to regional styles. The majority like to combine styles, experiment with dyes, color arrangements and designs, and more or less create something entirely different from what is normally created in the region in which they live. The resultant pieces are called general rugs. Another type of weaver who does excellent work is the artist who undertakes to create a difficult specialty, such as the Two-Faced, Pictorial, Sandpainting and Raised Outline products. In the better quality weaves, these rugs often command higher prices than the regional ones. Another often overlooked woven style is the Saddle Blanket. Hundreds of these less expensive, coarsely made, simply designed fabrics come off the reservation annually. Demand for these pieces remains fairly constant, not only because they are functional as horse trappings but also they serve as colorful, durable floor items.

The approximate breakdown of present rug production types on the reservation is as follows:

General Rugs 40%
Saddle Blankets 30%
Regional Style Rugs 25%
Specialty Rugs 5%

Navajo rugs produced during the Regional Style Period represent the craft at its peak of artistic expression and acceptance. Versatility and quality are high, with some experts claiming finer craftsmanship, color balance and design than at any time in the history of the craft.

From inception of the Regional Style Period the number of rugs gradually decreased. Prices began to soar in the early 1960s, with an annual increase at about 20%. Buyers were demanding quality, and only the talented weaver could realize the full worth of her product.

In the early 1970s, weaving was not economically attractive for the average weaver; many were not following in the avocation and others were becoming better educated and leaving the reservation for more lucrative employment. In 1973, in the Crystal and Lukachukai areas alone, there were only five name weavers remaining, respectively.

A spark of new life was regenerated in 1974 with the introduction and acceptance of the *Burntwater* regional style rug. However, by the 1980s, some writers, collectors (and even traders) were still predicting the demise of the craft before the beginning of the new century.

In the decade that has nearly passed, a resurgence has taken place that has production dramatically increased, artistic quality at an all-time high and prices soaring; the reason—commercial yarn and/or processed wool.[16]

The usages of these products in rug weaving are now entrenched in the craft and it is estimated that 80 percent of all rugs coming off the Navajo loom today are constructed with either or both of these material types.

Commercial yarn relieves the weaver of the tedious tasks of wool preparation (50%), thus increasing productivity and ensuring a greater profit margin. *[See time/cost ratio chart, p. 29.]* Other advantages include the multiple range of yarn colors, including subtle pastel shades. This wide selection provides the expert weaver with an unlimited palate of diversity that allows their talent and creativity as an artist to expand in fashioning elaborately designed products of excellent quality.[17]

But all is not well with this approach. The "purist" regards rugs made with commercial yarn as non-traditional, while the "modernist" claims convenience and the production of a more evenly stitched and aesthetically pleasing fabric in half the time. Some dealers and serious collectors will not purchase rugs made of commercial yarn and feel that unsuspecting buyers should be made aware of what type of materials are being used. Judges at recent weaving competitions argue that authenticity requires that a "true" Navajo rug be totally hand made. This includes the wool, which has to be sheared, cleaned, hand carded, handspun and dyed in a traditional manner. In some shows, where two rugs of equal quality in artistic expression and construction are being considered, preference will be given to the weaver who has prepared the wool.

Commercial yarn and/or processed wool is not new to the reservation. During the Late Classic Period, bayeta and flannel threads were used in combinations with Saxony yarns, followed by Germantown yarns in the Transition Period. John B. Moore was the first to see the benefits in reducing the steps of rug making. He arranged for processed wool to be utilized in the rugs that he sold and advertized the fact in his 1911 catalog. No objections were raised during these periods, nor in the intervening years when some commercial yarn and processed wool was undoubtedly available at the counters in most trading posts. The prevalence in modern times, however, of almost total use of commercial yarn is what some are predicting will be disastrous; that is, a complete loss of traditional wool preparation skills. This may be the strongest argument, for if the trend continues, a "real" Navajo rug that is procured from the back of a sheep, that is hand cleaned, hand carded, handspun, hand dyed and ultimately woven, will indeed be a rare item.

Change is inevitable, and the Navajo is adaptable. The reservation is now experiencing greater mobility, increased awareness, and with the old trading post system being replaced by Tribal-operated convenience stores, many aspects of the Navajo culture are becoming "Anglosized".

The Regional Style Period is coming to a close. Most of the rug style names will continue, but the geographic boundaries that spawned the period are now fused. What used to be identifiable patterns, designs and dyes associated with a specific locale are obsolete, as weavers are becoming more versatile in their creations. Except in a few cases, the influence of the area trader in weaving is also gone, and no longer does the expert weaver have to depend on the trading post as a marketing center. They now express their individuality and, if necessary, will travel hundreds of miles to places like Albuquerque and Scottsdale to get the best price. Arts and crafts dealers (and collectors) are in constant ploys with each other to gain the favored textiles from the name weavers, thus again bypassing the trading post.[18] Commissioned rugs have come into play, with recognized weavers offering their work even before the loom is warped. In short, quality sells and production is hard pressed to keep up with demand—at any price.

So, as the craft progresses into the 21st century, what is next? Acrylic yarns/nylon warp, mechanical looms, mass production? Many are hopeful that some intangible force will intercede and a rebirth into a "traditional period" might commence. What may prevail, however, from all indications, is an entry into a precarious "commercial period".

In any event, for whatever the future holds, history will always deal kindly with the spirited resolve of the craft. In its 300-year plight, it has survived three economic depressions, imprisonment of its makers, partial relocation and, what with borrowed ingredients like the Pueblo loom, Spanish and French sheep, German and English yarn, Mexican designs and American dyes, it has managed amazingly well in spite of it all. The rug came into being because the white man accepted a textile that satisfied his aesthetic needs at a particular time, and because of it, the white man has come to a better understanding of the red man.

The Navajo's love of beauty is reflected in the rug and perhaps the verse of the Navajo Ceremony, the *Night Way*, best summarizes the spirit of their lives:

In beauty, I shall walk.
In beauty, you shall be my picture.
In beauty, you shall be my song.
In beauty, you shall be my medicine.
In beauty, my holy medicine.

Chapter 2

FROM SHEEP TO RUG

Navajo Weaver and Friend

The Sheep

The Navajo people, lead a pastoral existence. They are "sheep-minded"; from sunup to sundown their main concern is for their flocks. The herding life is strenuous, especially in winter months when snow blankets the sparse grasslands, forcing herds into constant wanderings in search of food.

The "Navajo sheep" is not a particular breed. The principal flocks raised on the reservation are a mixture of various strains, including the French Rambouillet blood lines of the Merino breed supplemented with Corriedale rams. The dominant ancestry is still probably the old Spanish churro. The fleece is relatively heavy, yielding approximately 8-10 pounds per animal.

Shearing

The first step in conversion of wool to rug is shearing, usually accomplished in early spring when the fleece has attained its greatest thickness. Small portions of the flock are corralled at a time, whereupon the shearer will sweep a sand-cleared spot on the ground and commence with the flanking and ultimate trimming of the animal. Ordinarily, metal shears are used. There is no system to the operation, although a skillful worker will clip from the neck toward the tail, making efforts to keep the fleece in one piece. The select wool is obtained from the back, at the shoulders, and along the flanks. The remaining shorter fibers are separated and bagged for sale at the trading post.

Cleaning

Shorn wool, earmarked for weaving, is then hand cleaned of burrs, sticks and other debris. A fluffing technique accompanies the general cleaning and the wool is laid out for a short period for airing and drying of animal oils. Some weavers sprinkle white clay or pulverized selenite (gypsum) on the fleece to absorb oil and dirt which is carried in the oil. If the shorn wool is exceptionally dirty, a wet washing may then be necessary to remove saturated impurities.

Carding

The purpose of carding is to straighten the tangled fibers into loose, uniform pads. Small handfuls of the washed wool are hand fluffed and then raked across two hand-held, metal-toothed towcards. This technique combs the wool into slender fibers that can be easily spun. Carding also serves as a second cleaning. Persistent friction of the forward and backward towing removes most remaining particles of grit. Carding is the least enjoyable task in the rug process. It requires considerable strength in the hands and arms in an unnatural cramped position. Recently, more weavers are turning to commercial and/or processed wool, which can be purchased at trading posts.

Spinning

This process determines the strength and weight of the rug. The Navajo technique of spinning remains as traditional as the craft itself. No machine procedure is involved. Instead, a simple spindle stick and whorl, about 12" long, resembling a miniature ski pole, is manipulated with the hands. The base of the spindle is seated on the ground with the shaft twirled on the thigh with one hand, while the other hand regulates thickness of the fiber. Two spinnings are usually required to produce weft yarns. Additional respinnings will produce finer and finer threads, thus resulting in a more finely woven rug. If a weaver chooses, they can bypass the spinning step and purchase commercial pre-spun yarn, usually in a wide range of colors, over the trading post counter.

Washing

Before the yarn is dyed, it is necessary that it be washed. The only soap the early Navajos knew, and which is still preferred by many, was the high lathers obtained from roots of the broad-leaved yucca, mainly *Yucca baccata* that is obtained in central parts of the reservation and the narrow-leaved yuccas, such as *Yucca glauca* and *Yucca standleyi.* Both agents can be used fresh or dried and may be gathered at any season of the year. The broad-leaved yucca is the stronger, and more desirable of the two. After a thorough washing, including at least two rinses, care is taken not to squeeze, twist, or "wring out" the wool, as it promotes lumping and knotting of the fibers. Instead, the wool should be floated freely in the water and removed carefully and placed on boards, rocks, etc. for sun drying.

Dyeing

Various degrees of color can be achieved by the modern weaver. In some cases, a combination will prevail in a single rug. In the natural wool tones, such as utilized at Two Gray Hills, shades of tan, beige and gray can be attained in the carding step by blending desired amounts of black, brown and white wools.[19] In other instances, bright commercial synthetic dyes, purchased over the counter, can be used in addition to vegetal-dyed wools. If a weaver wishes to dye the yarn, it is done after the spinning and washing.

Vegetal-dyed techniques require considerable more time and effort for preparation of the yarn. Bryan and Young (1940, p.9) outline the following procedures for the dyeing of one color.

She selects an enamel kettle for dyeing, because she found that if she does it in tin or aluminum the acid developed in the dyebath while fermenting reacts upon the metal, and the color of the dye is changed. She measures out the dried prickly pear fruit and covers it with lukewarm water to soak overnight. In the morning she mashes it well, strains it, and adds enough more cool water to cover the yarn completely. She then places the wet yarn in it, rubs the dye into it well, covers it, and sets it in a warm place to ferment, having learned from previous experience that if she boils it the lovely rose color will change to tan. Many times each day during the following weeks she rubs the dye into the yarn. If she finds at the end of the time that the rose color is not as deep as she wishes it, she puts it in another dyebath of the same strength as before and allows it to ferment another week. She then rinses it thoroughly and hangs it up to dry.*

Bryan and Young (1940), follow with a list of ten basic observations that should be heeded in the vegetal dyeing of wool.

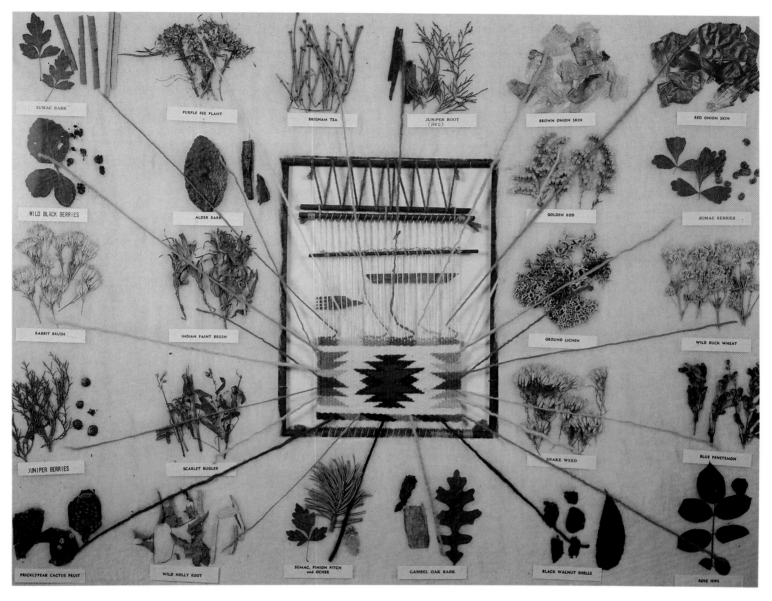

Display of partial vegetal-dye colors and sources.

1. The same species of plant grown in different sections of the country may give different shades of color. The shade of color may also vary from year to year from a plant grown in the same locality.

2. All dye plants may be used with or without a mordant. The use of a mordant deepens the color and occasionally changes it. The use of a different mordant, or varying the quantity of mordant used, also produces a difference in the color given by the same plant. Colors dyed without a mordant are reasonably fast.

3. Longer boiling of the dye with the yarn usually produces a deeper color. Occasionally the color is entirely changed.

4. Allowing the yarn to remain in the dyebath overnight deepens and brightens the color. It is believed that it also produces a faster color.

5. It is necessary that most of the dyes be boiled with the yarn to produce the color. There are exceptions to this, however. Cactus fruit, some berries and flowers lose their color when boiled. For this reason we allow the dye to ferment into the yarn as explained in the recipes.

6. The afterbath yarn, or the second yarn dyed in the same dyewater, is a softer, lighter tint of the same color.

7. Most of the plants may be used either fresh or dried. Fresh plants are usually stronger than when dried. Therefore, less of the fresh is required to produce the same color. Dried canaigre root, however, is stronger than when it is fresh. One must bear this in mind when substituting in the following recipes.

8. Dried barks, plants, and fruits should be soaked overnight before using.

9. Yarns must be rinsed several times after dyeing to remove the unabsorbed dye.

10. The yarns dyed by the following recipes have been tested for color fastness when treated with commercial cleaners and moth preventives and were found to be unchanged by them.

In arriving at colors in vegetal dyeing, the yellows are the easiest to obtain and range from bright yellow through greenish yellow to mustard to gold. The browns have a range from beige to dark-colored browns to deep rose and rich tans. The most frequently found colors are orange, gray, tan, coral, brown, yellow and variable tints of rose. A deep red is the hardest to obtain, as is a good solid green, both usually requiring additional color baths. Listed below are the 84 basic sources and colors found in Bryan and Young (1940). This is by no means the complete color range of vegetal dyes. The shades, tints, hues and combinations of plant colors reach infinity. The following examples form the basis of plant usage now generally in practice on the reservation. In several instances, one plant can produce several hues of color. This can be accomplished by controlling the strength of the dyebath (cooking time) and varying the recipe (amount of vegetal matter used).

Partial List of Vegetal-Dye Colors and Sources

No.	Colors	Source
1	Light greenish-yellow	Actinea flower, multiple-flowered (flowers and leaves)
2	Yellow	Actinea flower, Single-flowered (flowers and leaves)
3	Soft brown	Alder tree (bark)
4	Tan-beige	Alder tree (bark)
5	Yellow-green	Beeplant (leaves)
6	Greenish-yellow	Bitterball (leaves)
7	Pale greenish-yellow	Bitterball (leaves)
8	Mustard	Bitterball (leaves)
9	Rose	Prickly Pear Cactus
10	Deep rose	Prickly Pear Cactus
11	Light rose	Prickly Pear Cactus
12	Pink with a light tan	Prickly Pear Cactus
13	Tan	Prickly Pear Cactus
14	Coral pink	Prickly Pear Cactus and Mountain Mahogany (root bark)
15	Medium brown	Canaigre (roots)
16	Yellow-orange	Canaigre (roots)
17	Light canary-yellow	Wild Celery (flowers)
18	Bright yellow	Chamizo (leaves, twigs and blossoms)
19	Light canary-yellow	Chamizo (leaves, twigs and blossoms)
20	Mustard	Chamizo (leaves, twigs and blossoms)
21	Purplish-brown	Chokeberry (root bark) and Wild Plum (root bark)
22	Bright yellow	Owls' Claws (leaves, twigs and blossoms)
23	Light canary-yellow	Owls' claws (leaves, twigs and blossoms)
24	Mustard	Owls' claws (leaves, twigs and blossoms)
25	Dulled greenish-yellow	Oregon Grape (roots, leaves and stems)
26	Light gray	Ironwood (berries)
27	Orange tan	One-seeded juniper (twigs)
28	Yellow tan	One-seeded juniper (twigs)
29	Greenish-gray	Wild Purple Larkspur (petals)
30	Light greenish-yellow	Wild Purple Larkspur (flowers, leaves and stems)
31	Light orange	Ground lichen
32	Reddish-tan	Ground lichen
33	Yellow-tan	Ground lichen
34	Greenish-yellow	Blue-flowered Lupine (flowers, leaves and stems)
35	Soft reddish-brown	Mountain Mahogany (root bark)
36	Deep reddish-brown	Mountain Mahogany (root bark) with Juniper ashes
37	Rose taupe	Mountain Mahogany (root bark) with cactus fruit
38	Soft reddish-tan	Mountain Mahogany (root bark) with Cactus fruit
39	Dark burnt-orange	Mountain Mahogany (root bark) with Navajo tea
40	Henna	Mountain Mahogany (root bark) with Navajo tea
41	Light red-brown	Mountain Mahogany (root bark) with ground lichens
42	Light brown	Mountain Mahogany (root bark) with Alder bark
43	Reddish-tan	Mountain Mahogany (root bark) with Alder bark
44	Soft cream-tan	Mountain Mahogany (root bark) with Alder bark
45	Light brown	Mountain Mahogany (root bark) with Alder bark
46	Dulled tan	Gambel Oak (bark)
47	Light gold	Scrub Oak (gall)
48	Light yellowish-tan	Scrub Oak (gall)
49	Tan	Indian Paintbrush (blossoms)
50	Greenish-yellow	Indian Paintbrush (leaves, stems and blossoms)
51	Dull tan	Pinedrop (entire plant)
52	Reddish-purple	Wild Plum (roots)
53	Bright yellow	Rabbitbrush, large (blossoms and twigs)
54	Light canary-yellow	Rabbitbrush, large (blossoms and twigs)

55	Mustard	Rabbitbrush, large (blossoms and twigs)
56	Bright yellow	Rabbitbrush, small (blossoms and twigs)
57	Light canary-yellow	Rabbitbrush, small (blossoms and twigs)
58	Mustard	Rabbitbrush, small (blossoms and twigs)
59	Gold	Cliff Rose (twigs and leaves)
60	Bright yellow	Rubberplant (leaves, stems and flowers)
61	Light canary-yellow	Rubberplant (leaves, stems and flowers)
62	Mustard	Rubberplant (leaves, stems and flowers)
63	Slight greenish-yellow	Basin sagebrush (leaves and twigs)
64	Pale greenish-yellow	Basin sagebrush (leaves and twigs)
65	Mustard	Basin sagebrush (leaves and twigs)
66	Gold	Basin sagebrush (leaves and twigs)
67	Rich olive-green	Basin sagebrush (leaves and twigs)
68	Medium olive-green	Basin sagebrush (leaves and twigs)
69	Bluish black	Sumac (leaves), Piñon pitch, yellow ocher
70	Light oxford-gray	Sumac (leaves, Piñon pitch, yellow ocher
71	Light orange-brown	Sumac (berries)
72	Light tan	Mormon tea (twigs and leaves)
73	Orange	Navajo tea (flowers)
74	Light orange	Navajo tea (flowers)
75	Light olive-green	Navajo tea (leaves)
76	Orange	Navajo tea (leaves and flowers) and Canaigre (root)
77	Pineneedle green	Navajo tea (leaves) and black dyewater
78	Dull olive-green	Russian thistle (entire plant)
79	Deep tan	Russian thistle (young plant)
80	Rich brown	Wild walnut hulls
81	Gray tan	Wild walnut hulls
82	Rich tan	Wild walnut hulls
83	Light tan	Wild walnut (leaves)
84	Salmon pink	Brick-colored rainwater from red mesas in Arizona and New Mexico

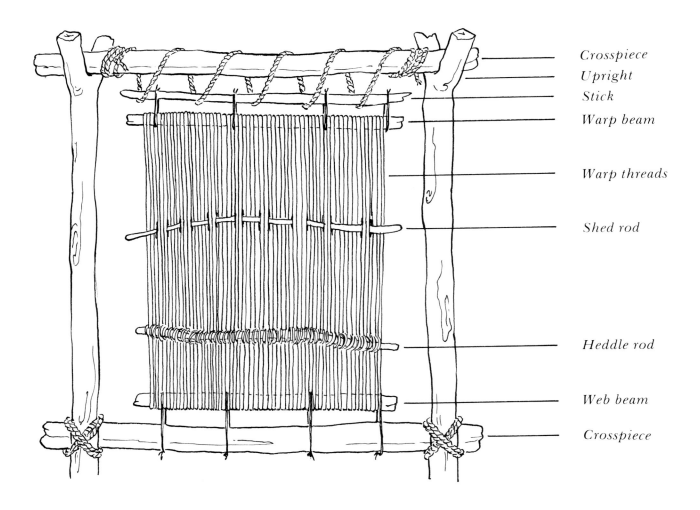

Crosspiece

Upright

Stick

Warp beam

Warp threads

Shed rod

Heddle rod

Web beam

Crosspiece

The Loom

The Navajo loom consists of two uprights and two crosspieces of log-size wood 6" to 8" in diameter, usually cut from small pine trees. The lower crosspiece, serving as the base, must be composed of the heaviest wood to support the balance of the frame. Legs of wood may be constructed at right angles to the uprights to serve as additional supports. It is very important that the entire structure be rigid.

Warping The Loom

When the weaver has determined the size of the rug that is to be woven, the warp thread is prepared.[20] The warp thread, or strand, serves as the foundation of the rug. It is necessarily stronger to support the total body of woven wefts. The stringing of the warp is done on a warpframe, a temporary device separated from the loom proper, consisting of two long boards forming the sides and two securely tied crosspieces (usually of 1" dowel or broomstick size) at each end. The warpframe is laid horizontally on the ground, elevated a few inches by rocks at the four corners. If there is sufficient room inside the warpframe (considering the size of the proposed rug), the weaver can be positioned within the enclosure and commence with the stringing.

The warp is one continuous strand that is wound in a figure-eight pattern at approximately 1/4-inch intervals around the two dowel crosspieces. Constant tension of the warp is maintained as the strand is passed over the dowel on the outside and returned under the dowel on the inside, thus creating warp pairs. The two figure-eight patterns created are called sheds, established by the insertion and tieing of two sticks, called shed rods, into the warp pattern. During actual weaving, manipulation of the shed rods creates the needed spaces for passing of the weft threads. To secure their equally spaced position on the dowel, the warp is then edged off by a twining cord to form a stabilizing top and bottom border.

When the entire warp is strung and secured, the warpframe is dismantled and the warp is transferred and mounted on the permanent upright loom by lashing the warp dowels, now referred to as the warp beam (upper) and the web beam (lower), with a lightweight rope. The warp beam is actually attached to another dowel, called the stick, that can be rope lowered or raised to desired heights. The shed rods are then untied, but not removed. The warp is straightened within the loom frame and a desired tension is applied to make the entire harness a taut unit.

Weaving

The basic Navajo weave is the tapestry technique in which the warp threads are completely concealed by passage of the weft yarn.[21] To facilitate passing of the wefts through the warp lines, the shed rods are employed. The upper shed rod is a loosely inserted stick placed between alternating warps. The lower shed rod (sometimes called a heddle rod) is secured to opposite alternating warp threads. By manipulating shed rod and heddle, odd numbered warps can be brought forward and separated from even numbered warps. To enlarge the opening for weaving, a flat stick called a batten (18" to 24" long, 1" wide) is inserted and turned on edge. The wefts ultimately are tamped into place by a wooden-toothed comb called the fork.

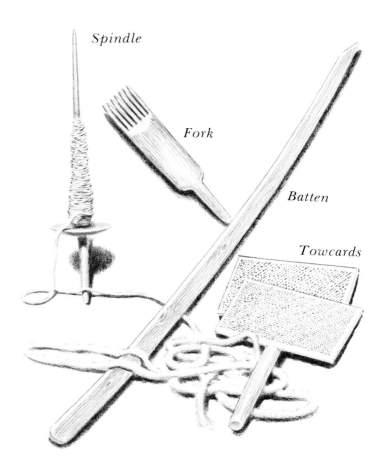

Spindle *Fork* *Batten* *Towcards*

The designs that originate in a rug generally evolve in the imagination of the weaver before the actual weaving commences. Traditional Navajo designs usually are handed down from one generation to another. As a result, a repetition of colors and basic motifs can prevail in a weaving family.

According to Bill Malone, trader at Hubbell Trading Post, a good to average weaver can accomplish approximately one square foot of weave per day.[22]

When the rug is completed, the weaver offers the result for sale at the trading post. Recognizing the value and time that was spent on the rug, they will understandably negotiate for the best price possible. If necessary, they will try several neighboring posts (or off-reservation outlets) until satisfaction is met. During earlier times when travel was somewhat restricted on the reservation, rugs were sold in proximity to the weaver's home. Today, with the ubiquitous pickup truck speeding along on improved highways, weavers may travel hundreds of miles to get their asking price. Considering this "roaming about" of rugs, it may be confusing at times to see a particular regional style, such as a *Crystal*, on the rack at Hubbell Trading Post, or a *Ganado* at Teec Nos Pos. For this reason then, many reservation outlets now stock a good selection of representative rug styles. If a purchaser is not aware of identifying characteristics, it is easy to be misled. One of the most common mistakes made in regional style names is to label a rug by the trading post from which it was purchased.

TIME-COST RATIO CHART (Sheep To Rug)	1973	Example: 3' x 5' Vegetal Dyed (High Quality) +	1988	Example: 3' x 5' Commercial Yarn (High Quality) *
	Activity	*Hours*		*Hours*
	Shearing (2 sheep)	2		0
	Cleaning	10		0
	Carding	40		0
	Spinning	90		0
	Washing	8		0
	Plant Gatherings (5 colors)	4		0
	Dyeing	40		0
	Loom Construction	16		16
	Warping The Loom	18		18
	Weaving	160		160
	Total	388 Hours	Total	194 Hours
	Probable Sale (To Trader)	$500.		$2,000.
	Labor (Cost per hour)	$ 1.30		$ 10.30

+Figures compiled through the assistance of John Rieffer, Wide Ruins Trading Post, August, 1973.

*Figures compiled through the assistance of Bruce Burnhan, Sanders, Arizona, November, 1987.

Correlation Chart of Regional

James, 1988 (this publication)	Rodee, 1987	Tanner, 1968
1. Shiprock	1. Four Corners 2. Red Rock	1. Farmington-Shiprock
2. Lukachukai	--------------------	2. Lukachukai-Greasewood
3. Teec Nos Pos	3. Teec Nos Pos 4. Red Mesa	3. Teec Nos Pos
4. Crystal	5. Crystal	4. Crystal
5. Two Gray Hills	6. Two Gray Hills	5. Two Gray Hills
6. Chinle (?)	7. Chinle 8. Nazlini	6. Chinle
7. Ganado	9. Ganado	7. Ganado 8. Kayenta
8. Wide Ruins	10. Wide Ruins 11. Pine Springs	9. Wide Ruins 10. Pine Springs
9. Western Reservation (?)	--------------------	11. Western Reservation
10. Burntwater	12. Burntwater	------------------------
11. New Lands (?)	--------------------	------------------------
--------------------	--------------------	12. Gallup
--------------------	--------------------	13. Coal Mine Mesa
--------------------	--------------------	------------------------

(?) Questionable at this time as to status as a regional style.

Style Weaving Centers

Bahti, 1966	Maxwell, 1963	Kent, 1961
1. Shiprock-Lukachukai	1. Shiprock	1. Shiprock
--------------------------	2. Lukachukai	2. Lukachukai
2. Teec Nos Pos	3. Teec Nos Pos 4. Red Mesa	3. Teec Nos Pos
3. Crystal	5. Crystal	4. Crystal
4. Two Gray Hills	6. Two Gray Hills	5. Two Gray Hills
5. Chinle 6. Nazlini	7. Chinle	6. Chinle
7. Ganado	8. Ganado	7. Ganado
8. Klagetoh	9. Keams Canyon-Pińon	8. Keams Canyon
9. Wide Ruins	10. Wide Ruins	9. Wide Ruins
10. Western Reservation	11. Western Reservation	10. Western Reservation
--------------------------	--------------------------	--------------------------
--------------------------	--------------------------	--------------------------
11. Gallup	12. Gallup	11. Coal Mine Mesa
12. Coal Mine Mesa	13. Coal Mine Mesa	12. Coppermine
--------------------------	--------------------------	13. Shonto- Navajo Mountiain

Chapter 3

SHIPROCK
'A Place of Deitys'

Shiprock—View is east from near Red Rock Trading Post.

The Post

The town of Shiprock (called Needles before 1848) is located on the San Juan River in extreme northwestern New Mexico. Its present name is derived from a volcanic neck called Shiprock, a towering igneous mass that dominates the landscape 10 miles southwest of town. In Navajo mythology the majestic rock is called *Tse Bit'a'i*, meaning "rock with wings," or "winged rock".

The origin of the Shiprock site dates from 1872 when Thomas Keam scouted the area for the federal government for location of a Fort Defiance sub-agency office. Plans for construction of the agency did not materialize until September 11, 1903. The first buildings were built of logs and adobe, replaced by brick structures after the flood of 1911.

The first superintendent of the Shiprock Agency was W.T. Shelton, a man whose contribution to Navajo weaving has been largely overlooked in contemporary writings. In 1909, Shelton conceived the idea of holding Navajo fairs, inviting not only Indians, but traders as well, to display their extensive exhibits of Navajo craftsmanship. The Shiprock conclaves, held annually the first week of October, were a great success. The principal theme was the presentation of rugs and silversmithing for which prizes were awarded. At the

Rug displays at Shiprock Fair, 1912. These rare and informative photographs illustrate several important facts.

Top: Newly, brick-constructed Shiprock Agency buildings backdrop the fair displays. Chimney smoke and smoldering bonfire ashes (both photos) suggest a brisk early fall day. Unexplained erroneous spelling of H.B. Noel's Teec Nos Pos sign ("EastNosPos") on the right. Note swastika designs in rug in the center—a John B. Moore favorite.

Bottom: The examples on the right, under the Two Grey (Gray) Hills banner, exhibit typical Crystal characteristics, which emphasizes Moore's contribution in the development of the early Two Gray Hills rug. The modern-day Two Gray Hills did not emerge until the mid-1920s. Note the Storm Pattern elements in the third hanging rug from the right, another motif possibly attributed to Moore. The Yeis had not yet made their appearance by 1912. Most of the displayed examples reflect Teec Nos Pos outline designs.

1912 fair, over 400 pieces of weaving were displayed. Publicity received for the Indian through the Shiprock fairs proved to be a valuable asset.

The first trading post in the area was operated as Robert Baker's Shiprock Trading Post. Bruce Bernard bought the Baker property in 1909 and operated it until his death in 1952. Another post, managed by the partnership of Walker and Hubbard, was purchased in 1912 by Will Evans. The Evans store was acquired by the Jack's Brothers in the summer of 1948, who in turn sold out to Russell Foutz in 1954. The holdings were transferred to a nephew, Ed Foutz, in late 1972, who operates the post today as the Shiprock Trading Company.

The Rug

The Shiprock rug type is called a Yei (pronounced "yea"). It was developed by Will Evans around the World War I period from stylized sandpaintings. The Yei is a colorful piece that depicts religious figures (a deity), but has no religious significance. The rug is often of small to moderate size carrying bright-colored, slender, front-facing figures surrounded by, in most cases, a multi-colored rainbow goddess that serves as a border down the sides and across the bottom. Additional designs may include interspacings of cornstalks and arrows. Backgrounds are usually white or light tan, with lesser amounts of dark and light blends of natural, handspun gray. The rug is finely woven with a growing use of commercial yarn. The Yei usually lends itself as a wall hanging in the same manner as a fine painting.

Another type of rug woven in the Shiprock area is the Yeibechai. Similar in size, bright colors and commercial yarn to the Yei, the Yeibechai is a bordered rug (sometimes incorporating a design) that illustrates Navajo dancers, usually in profile, impersonating Yei figures.[24]

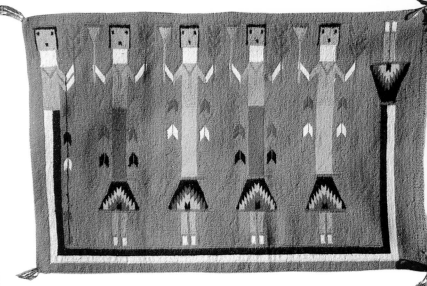

Plate 1

Plate 2

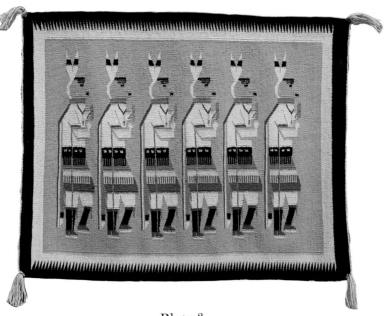

Plate 3

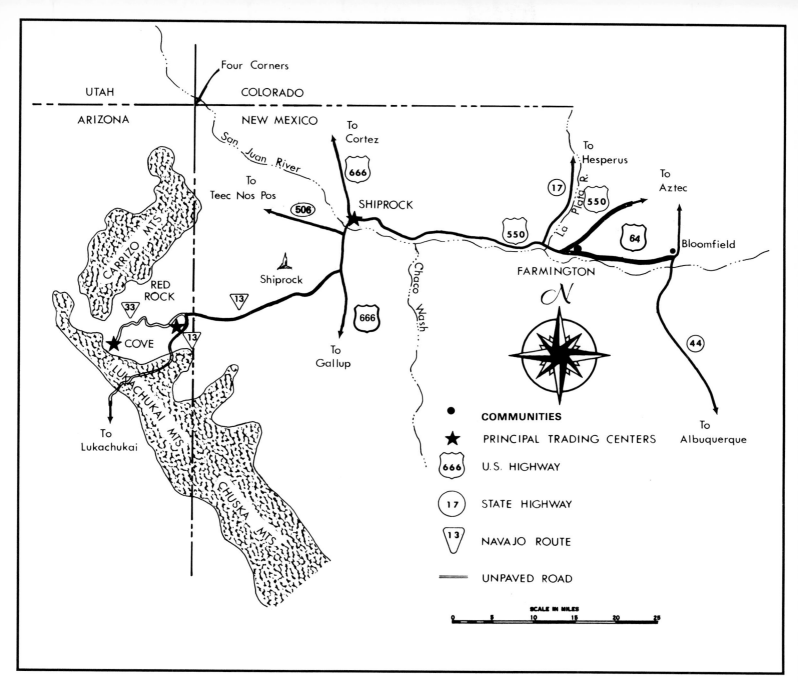

Shiprock Area Map

20-Year Comparative Costs					Weavers
Year	**3 x 5**	**4 x 6**	**6 x 9**	**Large Specials**	Daisy Barton
1968	$100-300	$350-500	—	—	Lucy Farley
1978	$200-500	$600-800	—	—	Mary Long (combination
1988	$800-1,200	$1,500-3,000	—	$5,000 & up.	Yei, Teec Nos Pos and

Trading Posts   Traders

Weavers (continued): Sandpainting weaver)
Marie Peshlakai
Lilly Touchin

Cove Trading Post   Raymond Ismay   Lola Yazzie (combination
Red Rock Trading Post   Troy Kennedy   Yei and Teec Nos Pos
Shiprock Trading Company   Ed Foutz   weaver)

Chapter 4

LUKACHUKAI
'A Summer Place'

The Post

Lukachukai is pronounced "look-a-choo-ki" and translates from the Navajo to "white patch of reeds extends out". The settlement is located along the west base of an impressive red-rock escarpment of the Lukachukai Mountains. The immediate area is one of the most scenic on the reservation. Transition from a sage-covered plain to forests and meadows is quite abrupt, leading some writers to refer to the highlands as the "Navajo Alps". The Indians call the mountains *Shiink'eh*, or "summer place".

The first trading post was established in 1892 by George N. Barker. George Washington Sampson, a veteran trader who managed a chain of trading posts, operated the store for a time following the turn of the century. Some references include the name Rico Menapase as being an active trader in the area, but no firm dates have been found to bracket his activities; possibly he occupied a brief time period between Sampson and W.R. Cassidy. A license transfer shows that Cassidy sold out to Earl Kennedy in October 1928. Earl's son, Kenneth, assumed managership of the store following his father's death in September 1971, and operated the post until its closure in 1979; the facility was later razed. The site, with only foundations remaining, is situated just north of Navajo Route 13 (1 mile east of the junction with Navajo Route 12) on a level shelf of land overlooking Lukachukai Creek. The lone remaining store at Lukachukai is located a short distance to the east where Bradley and Victoria Blair operate Totsoh Trading Post.

The Rug

The Lukachukai area is a second source of the Yei rug. Here, however, the products are of larger size, representing a greater use of handspun wool and synthetic dyes for color. Backgrounds are usually gray, red, black, or brown colored. In most examples the rug is bordered outside of the rainbow goddess, usually in a dark color. In many pieces, the rainbow goddess is completely eliminated, with a solitary heavy border enclosing the figures. More figures occupy the Lukachukai Yei, but are less detailed and colorful. Also, the Yei figures tend to take on a more human appearance, similar to the frontal-facing Yeibechais. The basic motif is the same as in the rugs along the San Juan River, but as those to the northeast are suitable for the wall, the heavier, coarse-textured Yeis from across the intervening mountains are more adaptable as a floor covering.

Plate 4.

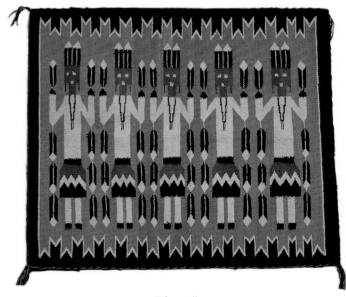

Plate 5

The Road to Lukachukai.

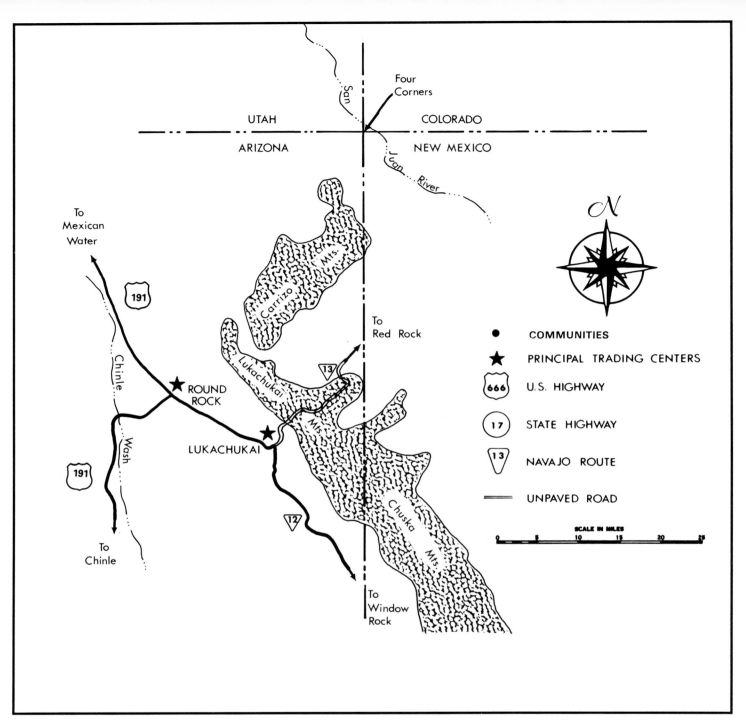

Lukachukai Area Map

Comparative Costs					Weavers
Year	**3 x 5**	**4 x 6**	**6 x 9**	**Large Specials**	Nora Allen
					Mary Bahe
					Grace Ben
1968	$50-100	$150-200	$300-500	—	Lucy Betony
1978	$75-250	$300-500	$600-$1,200	—	Rita Bitani
1988	$100-$250	$300-$500	$600-$1,200	—	Annie Brady
					Genevieve Brady
					Ella Gene
					Irma Higdon
					Annabelle Wheeler
					Lois E. Wheeler

Trading Posts	Traders
Round Rock Trading Post	C.E. Wheeler
Totsoh Trading Post (Lukachukai)	Bradley and Victoria Blair

Chapter 5

TEEC NOS POS
'Gateway to the Four Corners'

The Post

H.B. (Hambleton Bridger) Noel from Essex County, Virginia, was not a timid soul. He established his Teec Nos Pos Trading Post in 1905 in the remote area west of Shiprock, with full knowledge that predecessors had been chased out. He bought a high-powered Remington rifle, and after impressing the Navajos with his prowess on how to use it, he hung the gun conspicuously on the wall back of the counter, in easy reach.

Teec Nos Pos.

The improbable location that Noel chose was in foothills of the northern Carrizos, at the head of a cottonwood-lined canyon on Tisnosbas Creek. Furthermore, the bravery of the man led him into a region controlled by Black Horse, a Navajo headsman whose unrulliness had inhibited trading ventures.[25] Before a single spadefull of dirt was turned, Noel was subjected to a trial of several hundred Navajos who gathered at the canyon site to debate whether they should let this man with the corn-colored hair live among them. After a day-long council, the Indians voted to let him stay, for they respected his courage and it seemed that the time was right to link themselves to outside goods.

Noel traded at Teec Nos Pos for eight years, selling out to a partnership of Bert Dustin and Al Foutz and retiring to a farm at Fruitland, New Mexico. Russell Foutz of Fruitland purchased the store in 1945. The old post was destroyed by fire in 1959, and was rebuilt the same year on a higher shelf of land a few miles to the north of its original location. Today, Teec Nos Pos has achieved a community atmosphere and is a busy trading crossroads, mainly because its strategic location serves as a gateway to the Four Corners Monument. Unfortunately, the place name, "a circle of cottonwoods", which described the original canyon setting does not characterize the post's present location.

Noel's original Teec Nos Pos Trading Post, 1949.

The Rug

The dedicated weavers of Teec Nos Pos produce a tightly woven rug that has been described by many as the "least Navajo" of all the regional styles. The rug has a Persian flair, possibly influenced in part by John B. Moore of Crystal (*see Chapter 6*). Trader Noel took no credit for the design, and according to Maxwell (1963), credited a Mrs. Wilson, an area missionary, for directing the weavers in this style.

The *Teec Nos Pos* rug is very busy and intricate in design. Colors, often used in small jewel-like amounts, are rather flamboyant; bright greens, blue, orange and reds are popular. Commercial yarns are more often used, with some utilization of synthetic-dyed, hand-spun fibers. The typical *Teec Nos Pos* possesses a broad border that contains a design, usually in large H, T, or L arrangements. The rug primarily features a contrasting color outline of the main patterns which usually consist of zigzags, serrated diamonds, triangles and boxes. Because of its usually bright, multiple colors, the *Teec Nos Pos* is more difficult to blend into home decorating schemes. It is therefore more popular as a collector's item.

Fifteen miles west of Teec Nos Pos lies the trading area of Red Mesa. Here a small group of weavers are producing serrated, diamond-styled outline rugs that are reminiscent of the old "eyedazzlers". Usually designed with broad *Teec Nos Pos* borders, the wool usage is primarily traditional handspun yarns of grays, white, black, maroons and dark red. Some writers, because of the outline feature, have recognized the Red Mesa rug as a distinct regional style.

Plate 6

Beautiful Mountain.

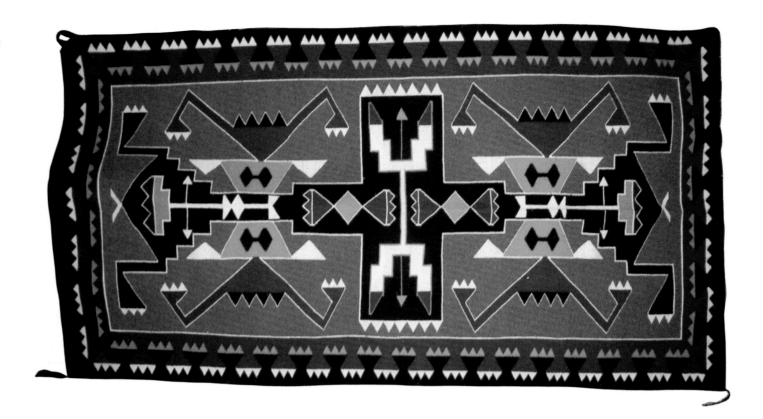

Plate 7

Plate 8

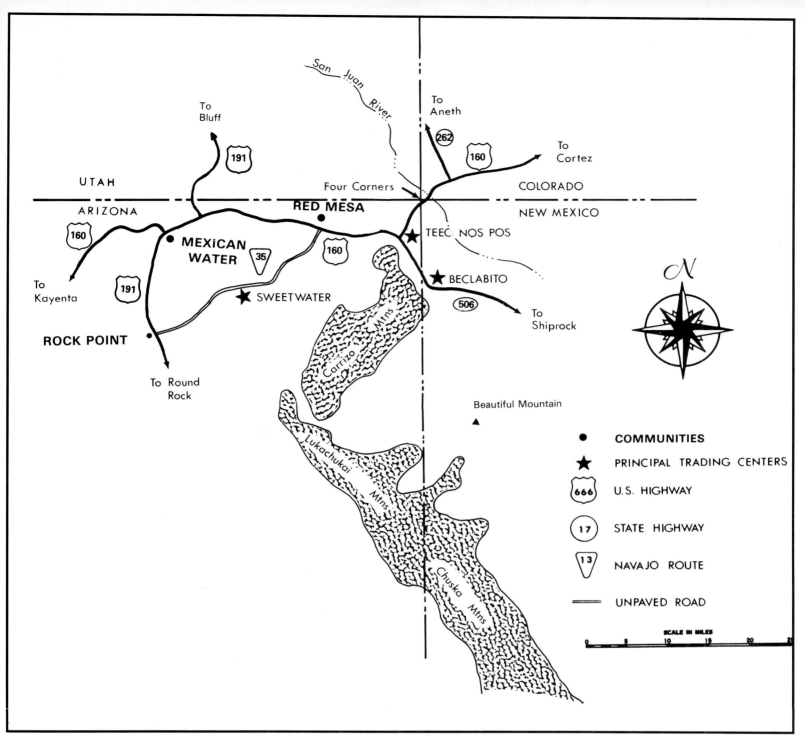

Teec Nos Pos Area Map

20-Year Comparative Costs					Weavers	
Year	**3 x 5**	**4 x 6**	**6 x 9**	**Large Specials**	Dorothy Begay	Lilly Joan
					Hilda Begay	Mary C. Joe
1968	$100-300	$250-500	$650-1,000	$1,500 & up	Nellie T. Begay	Alice Nelson
1978	$500-800	$800-1,200	$1,500-2,000	$2,500 & up	Louise Cattleman	
1988	$600-1,000	$1,500-1,800	$2,000-5,000	$6,000 & up	Mary Clark	
					Connie Yabenay	
Trading Posts		**Traders**			Emma Yabenay	
					Ruth Yabenay	
Beclabito Trading Post		Jay and Lloyd Foutz			Marie Wallace	
Sweetwater Trading Post		Wilbert Martin			Mary White	
Teec Nos Pos Trading Post		Larry Comer			Lola Yazzie	
					Mary Long	

Chapter 6

CRYSTAL
'Where Crystal Water Flows Out'

Crystal Trading Post.

The Post

On September 3, 1849, Lieutenant James H. Simpson, diarist for the famed Navajo Reconnaissance Expedition under Colonel John M. Washington, included in his entry for the day . . . . . *I noticed towering pines and firs, also the oak, the aspen, and the willow; and bordering the stream was a great variety of shrubbery, the hop vine, loaded with its fruit, being intertwined among them. Flowers of rich profusion, and of every hue and delicacy, were also constantly before the eye—upwards of ninety varieties having been picked up since we entered the gorge* [Washington Pass] *yesterday. Indeed we are all in hopes that, yesterday and today, we have been having an earnest* [view] *of what we may yet behold in this part of the world—a rich, well-timbered, and sufficiently watered country.*[26] Such was the description of the area the Indians called *Tonlt'ili,* meaning "where crystal water flows out". Here at the west entrance to Washington Pass, the only east-west corridor through the Chuska Mountains, lies the post of Crystal.[27] Blessed with a rare combination of beautiful red-rock buttes interspaced with mountain greenery, the location was long a favored campsite—but not in winter. *The mountain plain was very pleasant in summer,* wrote Thomas Keam to Interior Secretary Henry M. Teller in 1884, *but entirely impracticable in winter, as it is one of the coldest places on the reservation.* [I] *was told that eighteen inches of snow fell there on the last of April. Whoever recommended* [location of the sheep ranch] *never visited the place in winter when it is often covered with two feet of snow.*[28]

The success of early Navajo trading ventures did not generally include mountain bases. The seasonal handicaps were just too harsh. Some operations did well in summer when herders brought their flocks to graze the high country meadows, but deep snows which lay from October to late spring usually meant disaster. Several made a run at it though, including Archibald Sweetland who sat out many a lonely hour in a log post

Schili Trading Post, 1890.

Archibald Sweetland (fourth from left) poses in the compound at his stockade-type post high in the Chuska timbers. Late Classic Period stripes and bands are prevalent in the displayed fabrics, as well as a Mexican-Saltillo, serrated diamond-designed rug in the center. Note the tangling price tags, indicating that some sales force was in place. The man at the right is wearing a popular Chief Blanket shoulder wrap of the period. If color was envisioned, this piece would be a striking cloth of bright bayeta red (respun cloth) fashioned with broad bands of red, white and indigo blue checks. One interesting aspect of the photograph, recorded near the turn of the century, shows rugs that represent pre-Bosque Redondo designs and styles (1850-1863). While appearing to be well woven products, the unbordered motifs were not in the mainstream of other weaving areas at that time (i.e., brightly colored Germantown and Saxony textiles). Perhaps the remoteness of Schili and its area weavers inhibited change and innovative techniques.

called Schili located high on the west slopes of the Chuskas, 25 miles north of Washington Pass. The Schili site housed a series of owners before its final abandonment on November 14, 1892. Like Schili, Washington Pass was also a formidable location, but the east-west traffic in good weather warranted a greater risk. A Spanish-American from Fort Defiance, Romulo Martinez, was the first known trader in the pass, in 1873; Ben Hyatt gave it a try between 1882 and 1884; Stephen Aldrich and his partner, Elias Clark, lasted one season (1884), Clark and Charles Hubbell were trading in Washington Pass in 1885. Charles was a younger brother of Juan Lorenzo. Walter Fales came in 1885, and Michael Donovan took over in 1886, followed by Perry H. Williams in 1877. There never was an air of permanence about the early Washington Pass merchants. Their trading was probably from tents, and then only during the summer months.

John B. Moore, from Sheridan, Wyoming, was different. A slender, balding Irishman, resembling more the likes of an eastern schoolmaster than an Indian trader, he found the Chuska climate to his liking. He purchased the present trading site from a partnership of Joe Wilken and Joe Reitz, who with an earlier partner named Elmer Whitehouse, had traded at the location since 1894. Moore went to work; he cut and hauled timber from the mountains and built himself a log post; he freighted in supplies from the railhead at Gallup, and stocked his shelves with goods. The date of his license showed June 29, 1896. He called the place Crystal and he was open for business—and what a business it was! Moore endured the long months of winter isolation by employing Navajo weavers to make rugs for him. He originated designs, improved the wool for spinning, and encouraged quality weaving.[29] Almost immediately, he established himself as a master trader and businessman with a reputation for dealing in fine rugs.

He developed several motifs, some of which had strong Turkish or other Mediterranean influence. These style arrangements, in turn, may have been the basis for later regional types (i.e., *Two Gray Hills, Teec Nos Pos*, and the Storm Pattern). He publicized the craftsmanship of his weavers by publishing mail-order catalogs in 1903 and 1911. In a few short years the business was flourishing, with his rugs becoming known all over the country.

Moore's basic philosophy and ultimate success is best revealed in the foreword to his catalog, *The Navajo* (1911, p. 3-4).

THE NAVAJO Indian rug or blanket, no longer a mere curio, is now an article of real service so well known and extensively used that it is not intended here to go into any general and lengthy description of it. It is one of the writer's concerns that he has played a part in its introduction equal to that of any other; and firm conviction, that his part in bringing it up to its present high standard of excellence, so fully deserving the high esteem in which it is now held; is second to that of no other. Beginning some fifteen years back as an Indian trader in a rather small way, I have labored unceasingly with and among these Navajo weavers, inducing them to weave better, finer, cleaner and handsomer rugs on the one hand; and just as persistently on the other, to convince the buying public of the real worth and better value of this better product.

In the light of past experience, I doubt if I would enter again on the proposition if set back to the time of beginning. But once in it, have never been able yet to find a place where I could quit. It has not been easy. In the beginning I had stubborn and conservative workers in these Navajo women, and a discredited product to contend with on one hand; and on the other, a prejudice and lack of knowledge that has proved harder to break down and overcome than I had anticipated.

But, measured by results, I have not failed in either. My weavers are today making more and finer rugs than ever in their history, and their work is selling more readily, and at prices partially proportioned to its better value than ever before. Resistance, stubborn, hurtful, and senseless opposition on the part of the weavers, has given place to cheerful co-operation, good natured rivalry and friendly strife for excellence in their work. Prejudice and indifference on the part of the public is giving away to active interest and a substantial demand when and where ever my fine rugs are let in to plead their own cause.

Not the least part of my satisfaction in what has been accomplished is the greatly increased prosperity and better conditions of life that has come to the people among whom I live and work, as their earning power has grown. But, I am no philanthropist and must disclaim any philanthropic motives for my part in it. I saw, or at least believed that I saw, in their dormant skill and patience a business opportunity, provided they could be aroused, encouraged and led on to do their best; and a market for their product could be established. It seemed my one best business proposition at the time and I played it, realizing that if I would prosper myself I must help my workers to prosper too—if they prospered, that I would come in for a share with them at least.

And now, I am seeking your business on precisely this same basis and no other. If you ever should buy a Navajo rug, I propose making it to your interest to buy of me. For every dollar of your money that I ask, expect or may ever get; I pledge you full value and more than it will buy in like quality and quantity from any other. More: I promise you a quality that no price whatever will secure from another, unless it comes first from me, and at a RIGHT PRICE TOO.

This claim is not intended as a knock on anybody's goods. Any good Navajo rug is worth all you pay for it no matter from whom you buy it. But MY fine ones are a REAL and not a claimed specialty. They are in a class by themselves—no other has their like and there is no

A

B

C

Rug catalog, 1911

D

Design innovations of John B. Moore, suggesting here that some of which may have spawned later regional styles (from his catalog, The Navajo, 1911). (A) Teec Nos Pos, (B) Two Gray Hills, (C) Storm Pattern and, (D) a popular Crystal pattern featuring Greek frets. Note the frequent use of the swastika. This was called the "Whirling Log" design, which understandably lost popularity in the early 1940s.

By permission Sim. Schwemberger.
CRYSTAL, NAVAJO RESERVATION, NEW MEXICO.
Inside view of store.

Inside the store, 1911. John B. Moore (facing camera, on left) beside Manager, Jesse A. Molohon.

In front of the post, 1911. Manager Molohon holding Indian child; Moore, second from right.

By permission Sim. Schwemberger.
CRYSTAL, NAVAJO RESERVATION, NEW MEXICO.
In front of the store.

competition in them. There is just the one BEST quality, and that is the J.B. MOORE rugs, woven exclusively for him by the Crystal, N. Mex. colony of Navajo weavers. Our weavers are better paid than any others, but they do better work and that is WHY they do it. Our finest rugs may be higher priced than those of some others, but they are finer and better worth their price. And, you cannot get their equal from any other at any price, unless it may be from someone who first bought them here.

You are not asked or expected to accept my bare statement for this. See the goods and then decide. I will ship on approval and if you are not wholly satisfied, ship back at my expense. This is the kind my rugs are. I gladly take all risk of return expense for the chance of having you see them. A satisfied customer is worth more to me than any one sale. He or she, frequently come back with re-orders. At least, they will not turn

away from me friends who may want similar goods.

In 1911, shortly after publishing his catalog, Moore sold his holdings to his manager of three years, Jesse A. Molohon.[30] From 1919 to 1922 the post was in the chain of Gallup trading magnate, C.C. Manning. Manning's clerk, Charlie Newcomb, was an owner until 1936, followed by Jim Collyer (1936-1944) and Don Jensen (1944-1981). Al Townsend owned the post for five years before moving north to Inscription House, selling out to Charlie and Evelyn Andrews in 1986.

The Rug

The early *Crystal* rug of Moore's design was a bordered product designed with crosses, diamonds, terraces, a characteristic hook and fork pattern (Greek frets), along with swastikas and arrows. The Moore line was generously embellished with aniline red and to lesser degrees, outlines of blue.

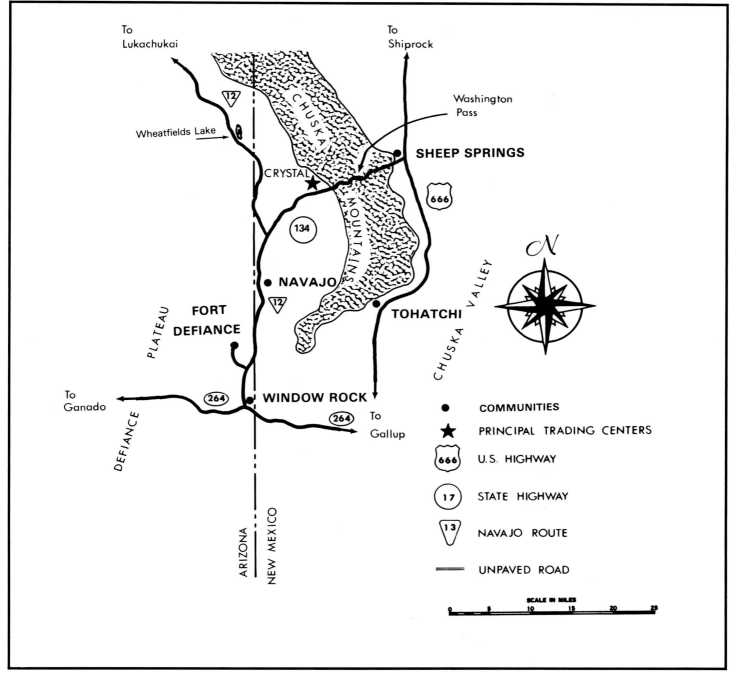

Crystal Area Map

20-Year Comparative Costs				Weavers
Year	3 x 5	4 x 6	6 x 9	Large Specials	Amos Begay
1968	$100-200	$300-500	$600-1,000	$1,200 & up	Margaret Begay
1978	$200-350	$600-750	$800-1,200	$1,500 & up	Mary T. Begay
1988	$400-600	$800-1,000	$1,500-2,000	$3,500 & up	Rachael Begay

Trading Posts	Traders
Crystal Trading Post	Charlie & Evelyn Andrews

Weavers

Amos Begay
Margaret Begay
Mary T. Begay
Rachael Begay
Irene Clark
Timothy Livingston
Mary T. Moore
Ella Rose Perry
Lydia Peshlakai
Jennett Tsosie
Mary Wingate

High Chuska meadow.

Plate 9

Plate 10

Plate 11

When Moore left the reservation in 1911, the quality rugs that he originated ended shortly thereafter. Some of his basic designs, however, continued to flourish for a number of years in the Two Gray Hills district to the east. From the grave of the pre-Revival *Crystal*, however, rose a new rug type. Dating from the early 1940s, the "new" *Crystal* departed radically from its predecessor, and, as it achieved public acceptance in the Regional Style Period, became extremely popular.[31]

There is no mistaking the modern *Crystal*. It is one of the most distinctive and beautifully woven of all the styles on the reservation. The rug is borderless and is composed of rich, all-vegetal, earth-toned hues of brown, biege, gold, and orange, with subtle touches of green, blue and maroon. Some natural carded grays are also incorporated. The basic pattern is Classic Period stripes and bands that are horizontally paneled and laced with an intervening, characteristic "wavy line" technique, an undulating effect created by alternating two (or more) wefts of contrasting color.[32] The appeal of the *Crystal* rivals most contemporary styles, mainly because its pleasing tones and simple patterns are so functional in home decorating.

Plate 12

Pony herd in Washington Pass.

Wheatfields Lake.

Red-rock sculpture near Crystal.

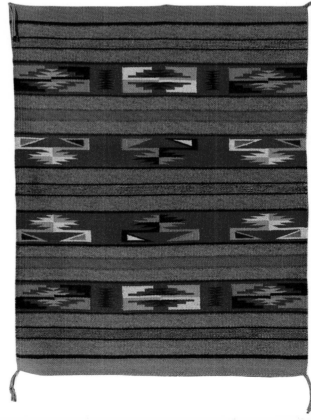

Plate 13

Chapter 7

TWO GRAY HILLS
'Beauty from the Chaco Desert'

Chaco badlands.

Two Gray Hills Trading Post.

The Post

The road is rocky coming in from the east and you don't actually see the post until a small rise is topped about half a mile distant. The first impression is usually amazement. "Is that it"? many have remarked, while observing the vast emptiness. "Are you sure"? Such is one's introduction to the home and place name of the reservation's most prized rug, the *Two Gray Hills*.

Plate 14

Situated on a treeless pediment separating the Chuska Mountains to the west from the Chaco wastelands, the site appears on 19th century maps as Crozier.[33] The name, Two Gray Hills, was probably derived from the Navajo, *Bis dahlitso*, which means "upper yellow adobe". Actually, there are several hills which backdrop the post and the color is tan, not gray.

In the spring of 1897, a year after he sold the Crystal post to John B. Moore, Joe Wilkin joined forces with Frank and Henry Noel and started a new post on the east side of the Chuskas. Business was a struggle at first, what with being located in an area where Indian customers were as scarce as blades of grass on the barren hillsides. Also, situated away from main travel routes, trader Wilkin recalled many long days at the post when he and the corralled stock appeared to be the only living beings on the face of the earth.

Brother Frank sold his interests in 1900 to Henry and another brother, H.B. Noel, who had recently come west for his health. In 1902, the trading venture passed into the hands of Win Wetherill. H.B. Noel stayed on for a while before striking out on his own into the Teec Nos Pos area. Two years later, the post changed hands again when it was bought by Wilkin's former partner, Joe Reitz.

In 1909, an Englishman named Ed Davies bought into the Two Gray Hills post with Reitz. A year later, George Bloomfield set up shop five miles west at a site called Toadlena, a corruption of the Indian name *Tohaali*, meaning "water bubbling up". With the collapse of Moore's rug dynasty at Crystal, some of his original designs filtered eastward through the snowy confines of Washington Pass to be nourished by Two Gray Hills weavers. The area women eliminated Moore's penchant for bright colors, especially red, and began to produce a distinctive rug of their own. By 1925, the basic style elements borrowed from Moore had disappeared. Davies, now sole owner at Two Gray Hills, and Bloomfield, were directly responsible for this, as they spent many patient hours instructing weavers in the fine points of utilizing undyed, natural wood coupled with quality craftsmanship. What resulted from the efforts of these two dedicated traders was emergence of one of the finest textile styles to come—and which continues to come—from the post-Revival loom, the *Two Gray Hills* rug.

Les Wilson, trader at Two Gray Hills, displays a rather large tapestry-class product (37" x 60") that contains a weft count of 85 threads to the inch. Woven by 21-year-old Charlene Deal, the exceptional fabric took 18 months to complete. It was awarded a blue ribbon in the tapestry division at the 1986 Gallup Indian Ceremonial, and sold for $16,500. With the exception of synthetic-dyed black, the remaining colors are natural white and six shades of carded brown, tan and gray.

Vic Walker followed Davies at Two Gray Hills in 1938; Walter Scribner had a partner interest in 1941. Willard and Marie Leighton purchased the post in 1948 and continued efforts of their predecessors in maintaining the quality and reputation of the rug. In 1972, the manager of the store, Derald Stock, acquired an interest in the post.

Following Stock's death in 1981, his widow, Patsy, continued to manage the store for two years before selling back the partnership to Marie Leighton. The present owner-trader, Les Wilson, purchased the post in early 1987 and the traditional concept of stressing high-quality, natural wool rugs is being maintained.

The Rug

The *Two Gray Hills* fabric is a bordered rug (usually in black), utilizing natural wool tones of blended white, brown and black.[34] With exception of the color black, no commercial or vegetal dyes are used. The designs evolve into complexities, with arrays of architectural groupings that focus on a center panel; lesser groupings are balanced in corners and along borders. Multiple geometrics occur in the rug with crystalline entanglements resembling patterns on snow-frosted surfaces.

Inch by inch and foot by foot, the *Two Gray Hills* rug is one of the finest textiles to come out of Navajoland today. It is also one of the most expensive. Small tapestries, delicate enough to be displayed under glass, have sold for as much as $10,000. One of the most attractive characteristics of the finer rugs is the light weight, accounted for by extremely careful carding and spinning, resulting in a high thread count in weaving. A weft count of 80 or more qualifies a rug as a tapestry. Some of the outstanding examples of *Two Gray Hills* rugs count in excess of 120 wefts to the inch. This is amazing when 50 wefts to the inch is considered a good Navajo rug.

A short distance north of Two Gray Hills lies a small trading area centered around Tocito (Navajo meaning "hot springs"). Here a small group of weavers are recalling some of Moore's early examples and have begun modifying the standard *Two Gray Hills* natural wool tones by inserting some synthetic dyes into the weave. Turquoise, or combinations of green and blue, appear to be favorite colors with the Tocito group; some examples reveal rust shades. In a subtle manner, the dyed yarn will occupy the center eye of the pattern with possibly lesser usages in the corner panels.

Plate 15

Plate 16

Plate 17

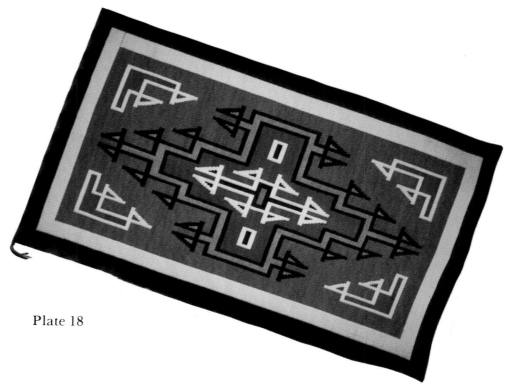

Plate 18

Plate 19

Near Sanostee (Navajo meaning "rocks around it"), located west of Tocito, another refinement is taking place in the *Two Gray Hills* weave. The Sanostee weavers are incorporating vegetal dyes to match the blended wool tones of the standard *Two Gray Hills* colors (beige, brown, tan and gray). This relatively new approach is resulting in some very attractive pieces. Some debate has been prompted by the Sanostee techniques, since rug "purists" refuse to accept the textile as a true *Two Gray Hills*.

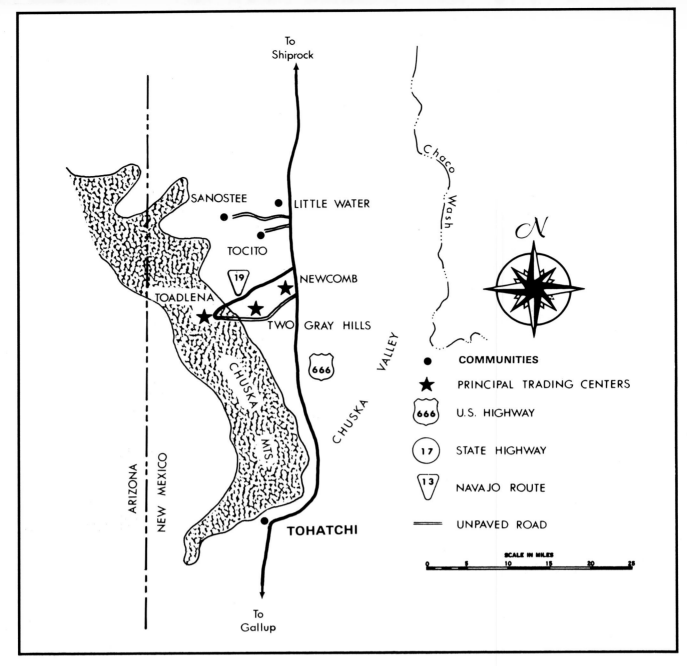

Two Gray Hills Area Map

20-Year Comparative Costs					Weavers	
Year	3 x 5	4 x 6	6 x 9	Large Specials	Elizabeth Billie	Rose Sloan
					Bernice Brown	Mary Teal
1968	$200-350	$400-600	$750-1,200	$2,000 & up	Cora Curley	Ruth Teller
1978	$500-750	$800-1,500	$2,000-5,000	$6,500 & up	Ramona Curley	Mary Tom
1988	$750-1,000	$1,500-3,000	$5,000-8,000	$10,000 & up	Charlene Deal	
					Julia Jumbo	

Trading Posts	Traders		
		Marie Laphie	
		Dorothy Mike	
Newcomb Trading Post	R.B. Foutz, Jr.	Rose Mike	
Toadlena Trading Post	R.B. Foutz, Jr.	Elizabeth Mute	
Two Gray Hills Trading Post	Les Wilson	Mildred Natoni	
		Clara Sherman	
		James Sherman	
		Margaret Yazzie	

Chapter 8

CHINLE
'It Flows from the Canyon'

Canyon de Chelly.

The Post

Since the mid-17th century, the magnificent canyon called de Chelly (pronounced *d'Shay*, Spanish corruption of the Navajo word meaning "rock canyon") has held special meaning in the hearts of all Navajos. A tributary canyon called Canyon de Mureto ("canyon of the dead") was witness to the Spanish massacre of a Navajo clan in 1805. Some 40 years later, Colonel Washington is alleged to have burned hogans in his

Plate 20

approach to the canyon, although the Navajos themselves may have set fire to them as they fled. Following this, in 1864, came Kit Carson's troops during the bitterly remembered "Navajo roundup".

The deep, thousand-foot chasms of the canyon offer protection; the bottomlands serve as excellent farms; the juniper and piñon-forested rims yield timber and fuel; and the soil affords limited grazing. The canyon has been sparsely occupied from about 1300 A.D. until arrival of the Navajo in the region (1600 A.D.). It was a natural site for trade purposes.

The first known merchant was a Mexican, a non-licensed trader named Naakaii Yazzie, who operated out of a tent in 1882 at an unspecified location. The first valid license was issued to Juan Lorenzo Hubbell of Ganado, and his partner, Clinton N. Cotton, early in 1886. Their site was at an abandoned rock hogan, which in later years became the location for Garcia's Trading Post. Business was poor at the first Chinle store and Hubbell let his operating license lapse the following year.[35]

Several traders followed Juan Lorenzo at the rock hogan: Michael Donovan in 1887, Thomas J. Lingle (1888), Bernard J. Mooney and James F. Boyle (1889) and John W. Boehm in 1889.

In 1900, Hubbell returned to Chinle and constructed a second post on a slight rise of land approximately one mile west of his original store.[36] Realizing the scenic potential of Canyon de Chelly, Hubbell built an elaborate two-story rock hotel to accomodate guests, with the floor level serving as the trading post. Hubbell's foresight for tourism was perceptive, but it was 30 years premature. The "no cars—no roads" environment of the reservation at that time forced a second withdrawal in 1918 when he sold his holdings to his partner, Cotton.

In 1902, a man named Samuel E. Day moved in and built a log store a short distance south of the mouth of Canyon de Chelly.[37] This store, a forerunner of the now-existing Thunderbird Lodge, was referred to by the Navajos as *aa dee kin ye*, simply meaning, "the big

house over there". In 1905, Day sold out to Charles F. Weidemeyer, who ran the post for 11 years before transferring ownership to George Kennedy in 1916.

Considering its traditional environs, Chinle was a desirable trading region, but not quite large enough to support three posts. It was a bit crowded to say the least, what with Boehm, Cotton and Kennedy not realizing much profit from the divided business. The situation was improved in 1923 when a tri-partnership of Camille Garcia, Leon H. "Cozy" McSparron and Hartley T. Seymour bought all three posts. They closed down Hubbell's old rock mansion and concentrated their business back at the two sites near the mouth of the canyon. Garcia eventually assumed sole ownership of the original 1886 Hubbell site and operated a successful trading business there until its closure in late 1985.

Similarly, McSparron bought out Seymour's interest in the old Day post in 1925. He renamed the place Thunderbird Lodge, and with Canyon de Chelly National Monument soon to be established (April 1, 1931), added guest accomodations and achieved Hubbell's dream of three decades earlier—a lucrative tourist business. McSparron held sway for nearly 30 years, building a reputation as a master host, reputable trader and promoter of Navajo weaving. "Cozy" retired to Sedona, Arizona, in 1954, and sold his interests to John Nelson, who continued the dual trader/tourist operation. Following Nelson's death five years later, his widow managed until 1964 when the facility was purchased by Gerald LaFont, who slowly phased out the trading business, concentrating wholly on tourism.

The Rug

Trader Leon H. "Cozy" McSparron, his wife, Nija, and Navajo patron, Mary C. Wheelwright, are responsible for the *Chinle* style rug.[38] Their experiments in the 1930s with vegetal dyes provided impetus to area weavers to revive the simple stripes and bands of the Classic Period. The *Chinle* rug has maintained this basic suggestion, and while generally considered to be primarily vegetal, synthetic dyes were later used to accentuate the smaller designs.

Garcia Trading Post, 1926.

Plate 21

Plate 22

Salina Trading Post

The borderless rug has a spacious feeling with small terraced designs and squash blossoms encased in broad bands. Some of the intervening stripes use the *Crystal* "wavy line" technique. The weavers in the district create an attractive rug of pleasing balance. Natural white wool usually provides the background, with lesser used shades of vegetal-dyed green, brown and gray. Rose colors and yellows are favorites, along with commercial dyes to denote outlines and termination panels on the ends. The rug is distinctive and well woven. Some of the better pieces must be closely examined to distinguish them from a *Crystal* or a *Wide Ruins*. One of the keys is dye utilization, part vegetal and part synthetic. Also, the weave is somewhat heavier than its all-vegetal neighbors. Today, there is a trend developing in the modern *Chinle* rug toward more use of pastel-colored commercial yarn.

A small trading post called Nazlini, located 20 miles south of Chinle, prompted a few arguments among rug experts in the 1960s. Some writers felt at that time that Nazlini area weavers wove a style that was distinctive enough to warrant regional recognition. The rug, known as the "Nazlini," was in essence an unbordered Ganado, exhibiting a combination of vegetal dyes and commercial colorants, particularly red. Prior to 1950, weavers of the district produced rugs exclusively in the Ganado style (red-black-gray-white). Some sources credit a missionary named Goss with influencing the Nazlini weavers to take up vegetal dyeing. The end result is that the so-called "Nazlini," being located halfway between Chinle and Ganado, actually reflects the style and colors of both areas in a pleasing combination. The basic design, however, is more aligned with Chinle characteristics.

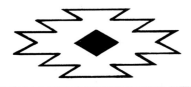

Sam Day to

1902

1938

1944

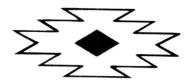

Thunderbird Lodge

1951

1987

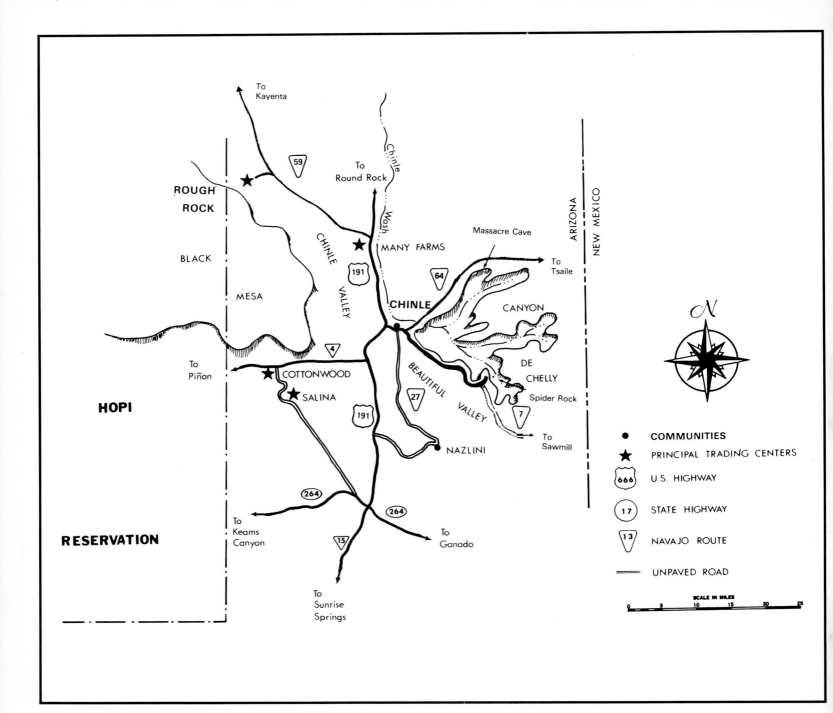

Chinle Area Map

20-Year Comparative Costs					Weavers
Year	3 x 5	4 x 6	6 x 9	Large Specials	Jessie Gorman
1968	$50-100	$150-250	$300-400	$500 & up	Ason Tsosie Hayou
1978	$75-150	$250-350	$400-600	$1,000 & up	Rita Hayou
1988	$250-400	$500-650	$750-1,000	—	Suzie Hunter

Trading Posts	Traders	Weavers
Cottonwood Trading Post	Ernest Gormon	Lorene Nez
Many Farms Trading Post	Claire Allison	Lana Spencer
Rough Rock Trading Post	Al Grieve	Elisabeth Stewart
Salina Trading Post	Dave Murray	Sarah Van Winkle
		Ella Yazzie
		Rose Yazzie

Chapter 9

GANADO

'Home of a Trading Empire'

Hubbell Trading Post

The Post

There was an aura of history and permanence about Ganado [Hubbells] that no other trading post could achieve. It was not only the long dim store with high counters, whose only light came through two barred windows at the front, it was memories of other times (Hegemann, 1963).

Ganado is situated on the crimson shale plains midway between the Defiance Plateau on the east and the Hopi mesas to the west. The main trading center is nestled in a small valley along the southern banks of Pueblo Colorado Wash, 35 miles south of Chinle.

The first settlement in the area dates back at least to Basketmaker III times, around the 8th century, and possibly even earlier. Ancestors to some of the Hopi Indians probably occupied the Wide Reeds site, a communal dwelling nearby, in the 13th century. The first trading post, called Pueblo Colorado (Spanish meaning "red village"), was established by Charles Crary in 1871. William B. "Old Man" Leonard also traded in the area between the years 1876-1878 before selling out to Juan Lorenzo Hubbell.[39] Hubbell, in honor of his friend and Navajo chieftan Ganado Mucho (Spanish meaning "many cattle"), is responsible for the current place name. From this headquarters,

Hubbell Residence, 1890

Backdropped by conical-shaped Hubbell Hill, this dwelling was built by W.B. Leonard about 1875. It was situated directly north of the trading post on the banks of Pueblo Colorado Wash. Hubbell (standing by tree), later built a larger, more comfortable home directly behind the store in 1900. The second Hubbell residence, which can be visited today, hosted scores of guests during its occupancy, including President Theodore Roosevelt in 1913 and 1915.

Hubbell Warehouse, 1890

A youthful-looking Juan Lorenzo (far left) poses with employees amidst a clutter of goods of the period. From left to right, some identifiable items include: bales of hay, bundles of wool, rugs, crates of Arbuckles Coffee, Dukes Mixture Tobacco, Gold Medal Flour, and on the far right, what appears to be sacks of grain. From the rafters drip stalactites of hides, harness and tack, saddles, ropes, brooms, a bird cage, and a babybuggy—a varied lot, indicative of the necessities of successful trading.

Hubbell Complex, 1904

View is south across Pueblo Colorado Wash. From left to right the structures are: (1) the first Leonard home, (2) multiple-windowed, north facade of trading post, (3) large, porch-fronted second Hubbell home, (4) massive-constructed warehouse, (5) storage shed and/or employee's quarters. Note white-washed privy sitting precariously on the stream bank in middleground.

The Home

The Bullpen

Juan Lorenzo, who briefly held a partnership with Clinton N. Cotton, built a trading empire which eventually encompassed 14 trading posts, wholesale warehousing and freighting. His reputation gained the title, "the greatest of all Indian traders".[40] Juan Lorenzo Hubbell managed his vast holdings for over 50 years.

The Rug Room

When he died on November 12, 1930, responsibility for the property was assumed by his son, Roman, who carried on until his death in October, 1957. His wife, Dorothy, continued the family managership until 1967. Hubbell Hill, a conical-shaped promontory north of the post, serves as the family cemetery plot, bearing the remains of Lorenzo, Sr., his wife, Lina Rubi; two sons, Lorenzo, Jr., and Roman; a daughter, Adele; and Many Horses, a Navajo family friend.

On April 3, 1967, Hubbell Trading Post was purchased by the federal government to be operated as a National Historic Site. It is an installation that functions largely in the manner which warranted its preservation—trading with the Indians. Today, guides conduct regular tours through the old Hubbell home, the post and surrounding grounds. Under National Park Service management, Southwest Parks and Monuments Association operates the post as a living history exhibit, a trading post carrying on the old tradition so well exemplified by Juan Lorenzo Hubbell.[41]

The Post

Plates 23, 24, 25, 26

The Rug

The famed "*Ganado* red" is perhaps the best known of all Navajo rugs, considered by most non-Indians what a Navajo rug should look like. Its creator, Juan Lorenzo Hubbell, possessed a philosophy that . . . *a good Navajo rug is like money in the bank.* He specialized in a well-woven product that featured a brilliant red background surrounded by strong geometric crosses, diamonds and stripes constructed with yarns of gray, white, and black. Hubbell's influence is still very much in evidence in the modern *Ganado*. The central motif is usually a bold diamond or cross, sometimes outlined in another color. Smaller forms occupy the remaining spaces. The rug can range from large, simple, bold designs to intricate, more sophisticated works. The deep red is still the dominant force throughout the fabric, although recently the tones have taken on rich shades of burgundy. In some contemporary examples, various shades of gray are replacing the red backgrounds. The average *Ganado*, while usually of area size, has a modern-day tendency to feature smaller tapestry types for wall hangings.

Although bordered on the south by vegetal-dye centers, the *Ganado* is a combination of natural colors (grays and whites), and the synthetic dyes of black and the characteristic deep, rich red.

Two areas identified with the *Ganado*, but sometimes subdivided into separate regional style centers, are Piñon to the west, and Klagetoh to the south. The familiar red-black-gray-white influence is evident in both. In contemporary weaves, however, neither Klagetoh nor Piñon has achieved the individualism to warrant regional recognition. Weavers in the Piñon-

Keams Canyon area (during the late Revival Period) became famous for their huge loom products, one measuring as much as 24 x 36 feet. Some rug experts felt that this size trait was sufficient to separate Piñon from the rest of the styles. However, in comparing early *Ganado* rugs, large sizes was also one of the chief characteristics.

From the Klagetoh "namers" comes further confusion. Located 12 miles south of Ganado, Klagetoh Trading Post achieved some measure of publicity during the 1960s from retailers calling a certain type of *Ganado*, a "Klagetoh." Here, the same red-black-gray-white rug prevails. Some current arguments insist that the "Klagetoh" is more sophisticated than the *Ganado;* that there is more design and complication in pattern; elimination of Late Classic Period crosses and diamonds; less red, more gray (particularly as a background color), and so forth and so on. Carelessness in rug naming continued farther when even the "Klagetoh" was subdivided. Twenty miles to the west, a post called Sunrise Springs found itself named in recognition of a particular serrated diamond-type rug—the "Klagetoh Sunrise." In all cases, the final answer was the imaginative mind of Juan Lorenzo Hubbell. His influence on Navajo weaving styles touched a greater geographic sphere than was originally considered.

In the 1970s, far to the north, at the gateway to Monument Valley, some Kayenta weavers were producing excellent red-black-gray-white rugs in typical *Ganado* designs. Some writers, or enterprising retailers, were apparently attempting to devise a new regional style rug to be called a "Kayenta." The only differing trait in the rug was its white background (instead of red) and smaller designs. It never caught on.

Plate 27

Plate 28

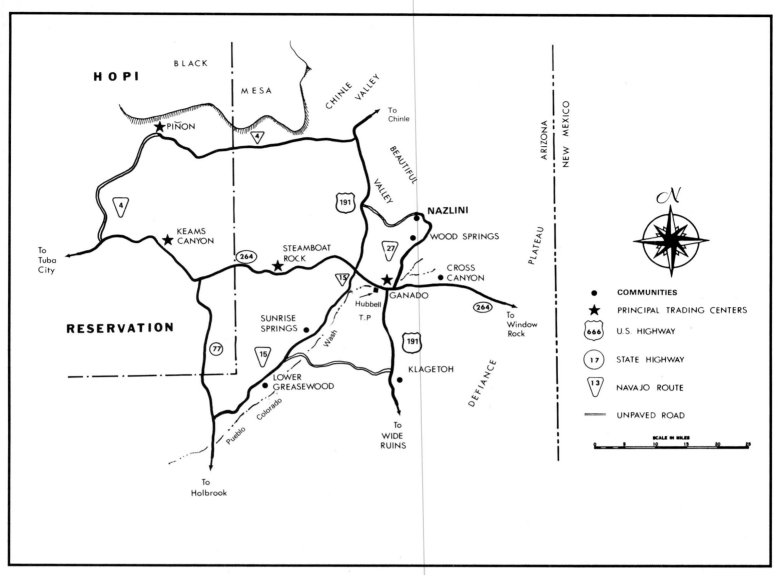

Ganado Area Map

20-Year Comparative costs					Weavers
Year	3 x 5	4 x 6	6 x 9	Large Specials	Mary Lee Begay
					Sadie Begay
1968	$150-200	$250-400	$500-750	$1,000 & up	Beth Bitsoni
1978	$250-400	$500-750	$800-1,500	$2,000 & up	Evelyn Curley
1988	$500-750	$800-1,200	$1,500-2,500	$,2500 & up	Mary Curley

Trading Posts	Traders	Weavers
		Lucy James
		Mary Jones
Hubbell Trading Post		Helen Kirk
Ganado	Bill Malone	Mary Reed
Keams Canyon Trading Post	Bruce McGee	Harriet Smiley
Piñon Trading Post	Ferron McGee	Patsy Roan Horse
Steamboat Rock Trading Post	Jerrold B. Foutz	Darlene Yazzie

Chapter 10

WIDE RUINS
'In the Hill Country of the Anasazi'

Wide Ruins Trading Post, 1973

The Post

In the sage-covered hill country separating the Chinle Valley from the Rio Puerco was located the trading center called Wide Ruins, named for the great Anasazi ruin, Kinteel, which means "broad house."[42]

Stillness best describes the location. The buildings were situated off of the main paved road and nestled in a sandy hillock that was hidden from the casual view by the low arms of spreading elm and cottonwood trees. Several, normally dry washes have carved colorful rocky swaths downhill from the sheep corral and serve as dividing lines separating the site from a more modern community and school on a hilltop to the northwest.

The Wide Ruins post was relatively new in the role of a rug center. Improved north-south roads connecting old U.S. 66 with paralleling reservation routes were mainly responsible for a series of 20th century trade centers that sprang up in between. At Kinteel, however, trading dates back to post-Bosque Redondo days, where a list of now-forgotten, transient entrepreneurs conducted their barters.[43]

The first permanent post, built of slab sandstone, was reportedly constructed by Sam Day (later of Chinle fame), probably around 1895. Whether Day actually traded at the store or not has not been established. The original post was built directly on mound heaps of an Anasazi ruin, which occupied both sides of a small tributary of Wide Ruins Wash.[44]

The trading area was enclosed in a fortress-type compound constructed of logs and tree branches. In 1902, another larger rock store was built on the opposite (north) banks of the wash where it remained in varying modifications for 80 years.

The recordable succession of traders commences in the early 1900s with the names of Spencer Balcomb, Wallace Sanders and Peter Paquette. Perhaps the most synonymous name associated with Wide Ruins is Lippincott. Bill Lippincott and his wife, Sallie, both recent graduates from the University of Chicago, spent the summer of 1938 as seasonal employees with the National Park Service at Canyon de Chelly. Succumbing to the love of the reservation the Lippincotts began to search for an endeavor that would extend their stay. With the assistance and urging of Chinle neighbor, "Cozy" McSparron, they scouted the Indian country for the purchase of a trading post. In October of 1938, they closed a deal with former Navajo Commissioner, Peter Paquette, for the then-called Kinteel Trading Post.

The Lippincotts deserve the credit for improving and publicizing the rug industry in the southeast corner of the reservation. Their insistance on the use of

vegetal dyes and encouragement of quality weaving ultimately resulted in a superior textile. Sallie kept on hand a plant recipe book which weavers could consult; Bill promoted a two-room addition to a nearby schoolhouse so that weaving classes could be taught to the younger women—promising to buy their class projects; and jointly, they conceived the idea of holding craft festivals which they hosted in their home, complete with refreshments, home movies, gifts for the children, and awards for the best weaving and silversmithing (Hannum, 1958).

Except for an absence during World War II when Bill served as a naval commander in San Diego, the popular Lippincotts traded at Wide Ruins until the fall of 1950, when they sold out to the Navajo Tribe.[45] A few years later the Foutz family assumed ownership and the post was operated by Phil Foutz under the banner of Progressive Mercantile. Jim Collyer, Jr., son of the former Crystal trader, took over in 1957, followed by a partnership in 1964 when John Rieffer bought in. In July 1973, the former sold out his interests, and the final owners, John and Sharon Rieffer, continued efforts to promote a high level of weaving excellence.

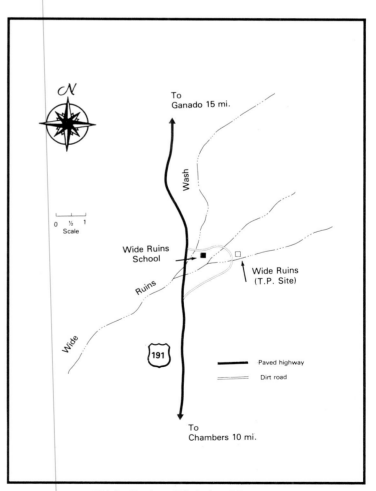

Wide Ruins Vicinity Map

Photo Album

Remains of original post, winter, 1946

Second store, built in 1902

Sallie and weaver

First stockade post, 1906

Outside the store, craft day, 1945

Bill and Sallie, 1945

Post from the south, 1941

Inside the store, 1944 Jean and Bill Cousins on the left (managers), Bill and Sallie facing camera

Remaine of Wide Ruins Trading Post, 1987

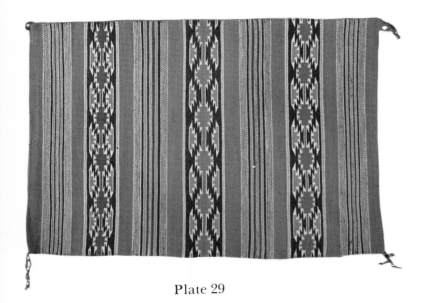

Plate 29

Plate 30

The Rug

The Wide Ruins district is the second all-vegetal dye center on the reservation; it is also one of the most recent in regional style recognition, being developed by the Lippincotts in 1939-40. The quality of the rug owes its origin to a desire of the traders to revitalize a poor rug market among area weavers.[46] At Sallie's personal preference and urging, the traders began their program by announcing that they would no longer buy a rug with a border. Undoubtedly influenced by McSparron and the Chinle success, they discouraged elaborate designs, and instead promoted simple horizontal stripes and bands constructed of total vegetal dyes and handspun wool.

The *Wide Ruins* rug that is still produced today continues in fine workmanship; all handspun, beautifully dyed and expertly woven. The natural colors of gray and white are used sparingly, but the blending of subtle shades of seemingly endless plant combinations, defies description. Soft pastels of exquisite pinks, yellows, beige, deep corals, rich grays, olive greens, multiple tones of tans and browns, and hues of lilac all combine to make the fabric a popular choice.[47]

To complement the colors, the weaving design is Classic Period stripes and bands situated across a borderless format. Overall simplicity is intended, although ornamentation is quite complex. Finely constructed outlines, hatch work, "wavy line" insertions, and beading techniques usually provide extraordinary embroidery arrangements. The panel designs are simplified forms of arrows, chevrons and squash blossoms. The subtle attention to detail and perfection in the designs approach a true artful expression.

As evidence by their product, Wide Ruins weavers practice their craft with the utmost diligence, always striving for quality construction and continually searching for that yet-undiscovered tinge that might lie in the dyebath of wild plum bark or the leaf of a chokecherry.

In some quarters, a division of *Wide Ruins* rugs is made. In the trading area of Pine Springs, located 10 miles east in the timbered slopes of the Defiance Plateau, weavers produce excellent fabrics that some buyers call a "Pine Springs." The argument is based on color—that the rug utilizes more tones of green, while the *Wide Ruins* covers a broad spectrum of colors. In the many examples viewed, there is a tendency for the color green to appear in wefts from Pine Springs, which might be explained by the forest setting of the post influencing weavers in their mountain locale. This does not provide a suitable distinction, however, to warrant separate regional style recognition.

Although the Wide Ruins Trading Post no longer exists, the design appeal developed by the Lippincotts and nurtured by the Rieffers, still lives. Most of the present-day weaver encouragement and marketing of the rug comes from Bill Malone at nearby Hubbells.

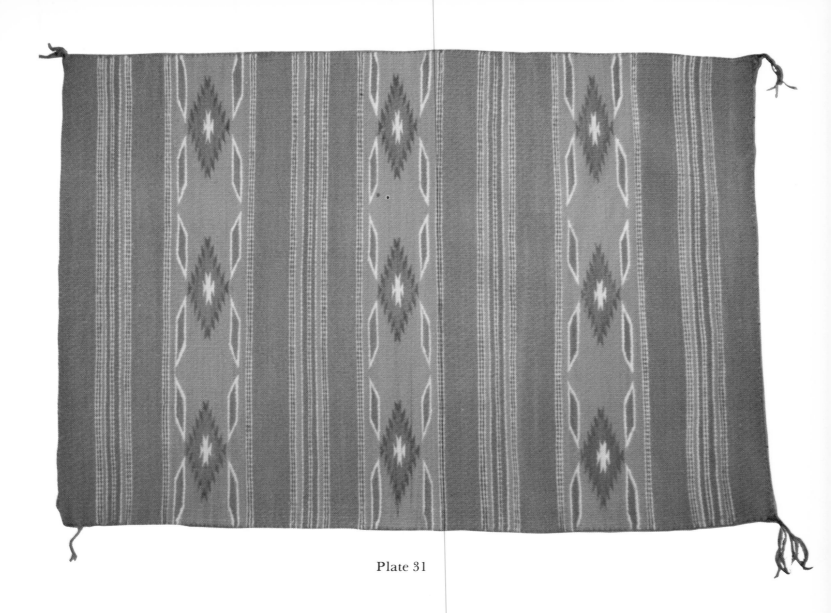

Plate 31

20-Year Comparative costs				
Year	3 x 5	4 x 6	6 x 9	Large Specials
1968	$100-200	$200-350	$350-500	$750 & up
1978	$300-500	$750-1,000	$1,000-1,500	$1,500 & up
1988	$600-800	$800-1,000	$1,500-3,000	$5,000 & up

Trading Post	Trader
Hubbell Trading Post	Bill Malone

Weavers

Stella Duboise
Lena Gorman
Etta Lewis
Rose Miner
Mary Nez
Agnes Roan
Betty Roan
Emma Roan
Geneva Shagie
Vera Spencer
Irma Owens
Cara Whitney

Chapter 11

BURNTWATER
'An Unusual Name ~ an Unusual Rug'

Plate 32

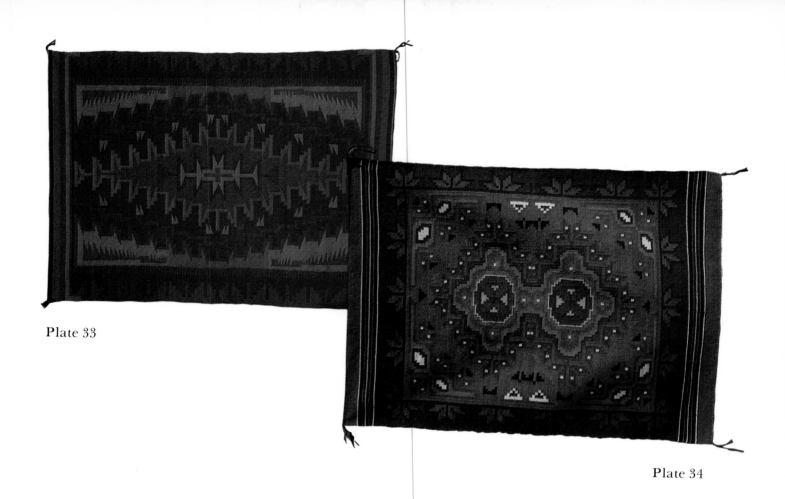

Plate 33

Plate 34

The Post

Shortly after the turn of the century, young Burris N. Barnes established a trading post high on the benchlands north of the Rio Puerco Valley. As the story is told, a ramada that shaded his well caught fire one day and the burned timbers fell into the water. The Navajos promptly named the place Burnt Water. The charred taste has long since disappeared, but the unusual place name has endured.[48]

Following Barnes at the post were Stanley Smith in the 1930s, Don Jacobs, Sr. (1967-1974) and E. Brady Smithson (1974-1983). Jacobs and his son are still active in the trading business and operate the Painted Hills Trading Post at Sanders, Arizona.

The Rug

It was inevitable that sometime, somewhere within the craft a "crossover" would occur between regional centers combining motifs and dyes. Don Jacobs, Sr. reported that the first all-vegetal dyed, bordered rug featuring geometrics from another area was woven in the fall of 1968 by a weaver named Philomena Yazzie. *Damnest thing I ever laid eyes on*, remarked Jacobs. *The weaver had done a good job on the rug, as I recall, but we were sort of used to Wide Ruins types around here. I didn't think it would go at first, being as how it looked like a pale Ganado, but it sold right away. This rug business is funny sometimes.* From that point in time, the *Burntwater* regional style was born.[49]

Jacobs continued to encourage the practice, suggesting vegetal dyeing of design features primarily from *Ganado* and *Two Gray Hills* types. By the early 1970s, area weavers were turning almost exclusively to producing this rug style. Its reputation and appeal was further enhanced by coverage in the July 1974 issue of *Arizona Highways Magazine*. The timing of the *Burntwater's* popularity was fortunately coincidental with a struggling time for the craft, and it added a welcome new stimulus to the industry.

The *Burntwater* rug can be divided into an early and late phase. As previously mentioned, its initial development featured *Ganado* and *Two Gray Hills* designs that were woven with only a few muted shades of vegetal-dyed, handspun yarn (**Plate 33**). In the early 1980s, principally through the efforts of Bill Malone at Hubbells and Bruce Burnham at nearby Sanders, Arizona, the modern *Burntwater* has now achieved its own identity. It has exploded into a pastel rainbow of color usage. Constructed primarily of vegetal-dyed commercial yarn, the profusely decorated schemes have included more than 25 separate hues counted in one rug.[50] Also, the design arrangements are much more complex, featuring outlined intricate groupings that exhibit the artistic flair of a Persian tapestry (**Plate 34**). The rug is well woven and beautifully balanced within strong outside borders, and in some examples, multiple inner borders. Some weavers have retained *Wide Ruins* features by continuing to incorporate horizontal bands as end panels (**Plate 35**).

Plate 35

Plate 36

Plate 37

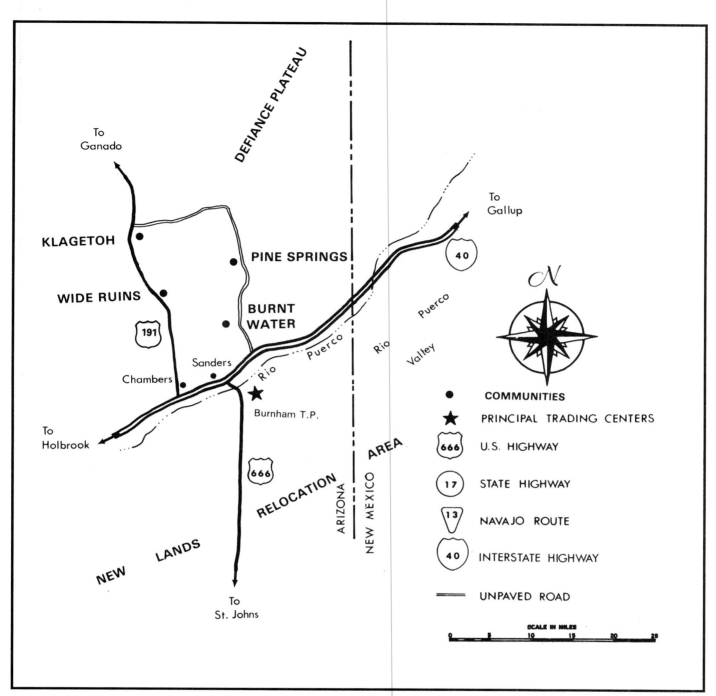

Burnt Water Area Map

20-Year Comparative Costs					Weavers
Year	3 x 5	4 x 6	6 x 9	Large Specials	Bah Yazzie Ashley
					Roselyn Begay
1968	—	—	—	—	Stabley Begay
1978	$800-2,000	$2,500-5,000	$6,500-8,000	—	Winnie James
1988	$1,200-3,000	$4,000-6,000	$8,000-$10,000	$12,000 & up	Bruce Nez
					Brenda Spencer

Trading Post	Trader	Andrea Yazzie
Burnham Trading Post, Sanders, Arizona	Bruce Burnham	Larry Yazzie
		Philomena Yazzie

Chapter 12

NEW LANDS
'A New Beginning'

Herding on new lands.

Historical Development

Coal Mine Mesa is located on the Hopi Indian Reservation about 25 miles southeast of Tuba City, Arizona. A rug of the same name, which carried a raised outline feature, enjoyed a brief period of regional style recognition in the 1950s and early 1960s. Developed by the late Ned Hatathi as a Navajo Arts and Crafts Guild project, the textile represented more of a weaving technique than a style piece.[55] Through a manipulation of the weft and warp threads, various selected patterns could be slightly raised, and when outlined in a contrasting color, gave the design a three-dimensional effect.[56] The raised outline appeared on but one side, thus giving the rug the distinction of having a front and back surface. The raised outline technique soon spread to other parts of the reservation, and coupled with the closing of the trading post at Coal Mine Mesa in 1968, the regional influence of the style was lost. The weave has remained popular, however, even into the modern era where it has prevailed as a specialty rug, and at times has been incorporated into other styles (i.e., "raised outline Yei", "raised outline Storm Pattern", etc.).

In the wake of the Navajo-Hopi Land Dispute, many Navajo families were relocated to other parts of the reservation.[57] This included 500 families who were resettled on new lands (hence the name) recently purchased by the Tribe, south and east of Sanders, Arizona.[58] (*See Burnt Water area map.*) In 1982, principally through the promotions of Bruce Burnham at Sanders, Bill Malone of Hubbell Trading Post, and Bruce McGee at Keams Canyon, the raised outline rug has resurfaced through the efforts of former Coal Mine Mesa weavers, and has manifested itself into an entirely new style. Called *New Lands*, its evolution is born of combinations and techniques borrowed from other types, which is acceptable as the success of Navajo weaving has always depended on the flexibility to adapt and utilize other innovations.

Plate 39

Plate 38

The Rug

The *New Lands* is basically a composite textile of *Teec Nos Pos* designs that is constructed of vegetal-dyed commercial yarn and features the raised outline technique. Being vegetal, its palate is soft pastels and differs in that respect from the brightly colored, parent rug of the Four Corners area. It is extremely popular at this time, due principally to its limited production, excellent weave, design appeal and decorator colors, as well as featuring the desirable raised outline. Because of its newness, it is also receiving attention at arts and crafts shows, from museum procurers, and from dealers and collectors. Prices are running slightly higher than for a comparable *Burntwater*. Some *Burntwater* designs are also being constructed in the raised outline format, but because of fewer geometrics required in the design, are less expensive. Only time and the desire of "aficionados" will determine and judge the future of the *New Lands* raised outline.

20-Year Comparative Costs					Weavers
Year	3 x 5	4 x 6	6 x 9	Large Specials	Andrew Begay
					Keith Begay
1968	—	—	—	—	Mary Begay
1978	—	—	—	—	Stanley Begay
1988	$2,000-3,500	$4,500-7,000	$8,500-$12,000	$15,000 & up	Wanda Begay
					Sarah Tsinnie
					Janet Tsinnie

Trading Post	Trader	
Burnham Trading Post, Sanders, Arizona	Bruce Burnham	

Chapter 13

WESTERN RESERVATION

Plate 40

Winter silhouette, Monument Valley.

Red Lake

'On the Rainbow Trail'

The Post

The Red Lake Trading Post at Tonalea, Navajo meaning "where water comes together", is said to be the birthplace of the reservation's most controversial and interestingly designed rug—the Storm Pattern.

Situated halfway down the slope of a sandy mesa, with environs strongly resembling a desert of the Far East, the trading post was named for a shallow expanse of land that is only a "lake" during wet years. The best thing about Red Lake, and it is argumentative, is the view to the east where Black Mesa breaks the rather desolate, unattractive foreground. Rattlesnakes thrived and loved the place. Trader Johnny O'Farrell (1918-1935) killed them by the hordes during spring and summer months. Johnny's wife, Cora, gained more than a local reputation by serving her "special tuna sandwiches" to passing tourists. It was said that she always enjoyed watching the visitors gag a bit, when told it was freshly boiled rattlesnake meat. Equally interesting was Cora's favorite piece of jewelry—a threaded necklace of a rattlesnake's spinal column.

Red Lake Trading Post was established in 1881, in the northwest corner of the Hopi Reservation, by Joseph H. Lee, son of John Doyle Lee of Lee's Ferry fame. The post was situated at two different sites prior to its final location. Lee's original store, a canvas-topped shack, was two miles down the wash to the southwest. In 1885, George McAdams moved the store back to the east, along the south shore of the "lake". In 1888, McAdams sold out to a Dutchman named Dittenhoffer. "Ditt," as he was called, was killed in a lover's quarrel at the post in 1890. His principal creditor, Charles Babbitt of Babbitt Brothers Trading Company of Flagstaff, assumed active control of the post a year later, and moved the operation to its present rock-constructed, two-story quarters in 1891.[51]

The post functioned as a company-operated enterprise. Babbitt Brothers, who owned a chain of trading posts on the Navajo and Hopi reservations, initiated their business through a resident manager-trader arrangement with partnership privileges. Beginning in 1891, with a first manager named Sam Preston, the

The desert setting of Red Lake Trading Post at Tonalea, 1949. View is south across dried-up lake flats toward Black Mesa on the horizon.

Plate 41

The contemporary Storm Pattern, although still very much in evidence in western sectors, is now being found throughout the reservation. Beautiful examples are woven in most areas and sometimes display characteristics of the local regional style. Even vegetal-dyed Storm Patterns can be found on racks.[53]

The origin of the Storm Pattern has prompted considerable debate. The general inclination is to consider it symbolic, although the symbolism appears to have been conceived by a white man. The traditional sales factor in describing the alleged "sacredness" of the rug is that the center square is the hogan, or "center of the world," and that the four squares at each of the corners represent the four sacred mountains of Navajo mythology.[54] The connecting lines, usually zigzagged, are intended as lightning bolts carrying blessings to and fro between the squares, thus bestowing good spirits on the weaver's household.

Some writers credit an early trader with devising the Storm Pattern. Others say that it is a variation of a commercial design that appeared on flour sacks being shipped out of Flagstaff at the turn of the century. In *Navajo Trading Days*, Hegemann (1963) portrays a rug that displays all of the standard features of a contemporary Storm Pattern. Her description reads: *A typical and popular rug pattern woven in the district of Western Navajo between Kayenta and Tuba. Many of the good weavers of the Tsayutcissi family used this design of the Four Mountains bordering the Navajo World with the lake in the middle, and the Sacred Arrows, and Whirling Logs. This was called the Red Lake pattern because a trader at that post had originated the design sometime after 1900.*

Another possibility would seem to rest with the imaginative brain of John B. Moore of Crystal. Moore was continually involved with design innovations; pictured in his mail order catalog, *The Navajo* (1911), is a perfect example of a modern-day Storm Pattern. Moore called this his ER-20 Class, "special design rug", and noted that. . . *it is legendary in Navajo mythology and not many weavers will do it for superstitious reasons.* Considering that passage, it would appear that Mr. Moore's design abilities were possibly exceeded by his salesmanship.

West Mitten, Monument Valley.

succession of employees have been: H.K. Warren (1897-1905), Earl Boyer (1905-1918), Johnny O'Farrell (1918-1935), Floyd Boyle (1935-1953), Coit Patterson (1953-1955), Harold Lockhart (1955-1973), and Jerry Norris (1973-1987).[52]

One of the more interesting sidelights to the old post were the periodic visits of the noted author, Zane Grey. Grey, seemingly quite taken with the northwest corner of the Indian country, was the guest of trader Earl Boyer on several occasions between 1911-1914 while gathering material for the *Rainbow Trail* (1915). The first chapter of the book is set at Red Lake Trading Post.

The Rug

The basic design of the Storm Pattern is a bordered rug that is highly symmetrical, displaying certain standard features. Always there is a square or rectangular center from which radiating lines lead to the four corners, where additional squares are set. Secondary elements may include zigzags, diamonds, arrows, and stepped terraces serving as fillers along the borders. The rug tends to be elongated in shape to facilitate connecting lines between the rectangular designs. Weavers of the Storm Pattern work primarily in commercial dyes of red-black-gray-white combinations.

PLATE XXVIII
Special Design and Weave by "Dug-gau-eth-lun bi Dazhie."

From "ER-20" class, original 64x92 inches in size. This pattern is one of the really legendary designs embodying a portion of the Navajo mythology. Not many weavers will do it for superstitious reasons and on that account its production is practically confined to one family or clan. It is an improved adaptation of Plate IX, also originated by this same woman, and done in red, white and black. She, and her immediate relatives, have been making it as shown here for two or three years past, and the rug has never failed to satisfy when shown to a prospective buyer. The trouble has been to get enough of them made, and to overcome this is the main purpose of this engraving. With the pattern for a working model, we hope to get other weavers to making it.

"ER-20" class, size 45x75 inches up to 6x9 feet and price, 90c to $1.00 per square foot, or $21.00 to $23.50 for small, and up or down, according to size. Made to order in any size and colors desired at price in proportion to size, but the colors shown can hardly be improved upon.

Very rarely done in the "T-XX" class, but at $1.00 to $2.00 per lb., if we should chance to have any. Not made to order in this class.

John B. Moore's "special design rug"—a forerunner to the modern-day Storm Pattern.

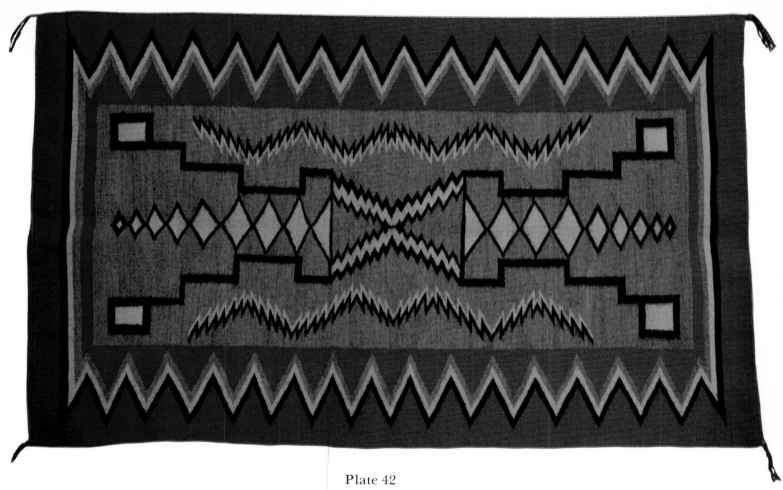

Plate 42

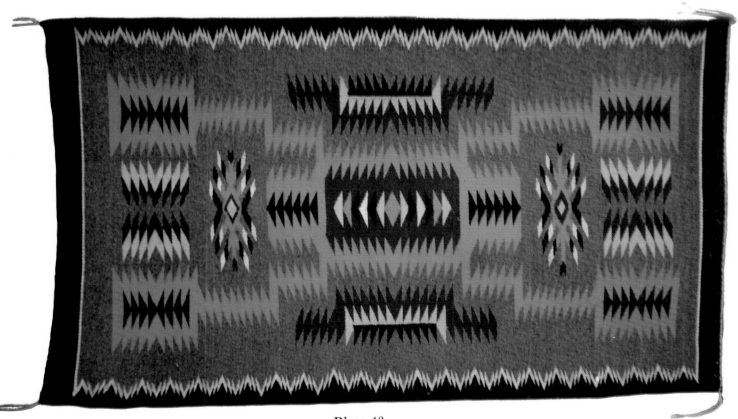

Plate 43

Shonto

'Place of Sunlight Water'

Shonto Trading Post.

Trader Trolet and family, 1987.

Shonto Trading Post, 1932.

The Post

A Southwestern Shangri-la, the remote trading post of Shonto deserves some mention, for there is no other place on the Navajo Reservation that retains the integrity of the early days of Indian trading as the *place in the canyon. (See title page sketch.)* A *primitive place* where few roads enter and, until a short time ago, only Navajo was the spoken language and trade goods were known by pictures on wrappers, not by printed labels. An *isolated place* where electricity was the last to reach, the nearest phone was 25 miles away, and where ponies and wagons were more valued and practical than pickup trucks. A *small place*, not ambitious in motive nor attitude, where some traders could break even on five hides a day, a few good saddle blankets and an occasional bumper crop of piñons. And finally, an *amazingly picturesque place*—a gem setting in the fall when gold leaves of the cottonwood grove contrast brilliantly against a backdrop of 200-foot salmon-pink cliffs.

First out of a tent, then a one-room rock store, Joe Lee developed the site in 1914 along the base of the east wall of Shonto Canyon—a ten-mile, non-river gorge that carries runoffs from snowmelts and summer thunderstorms. The post owes its existence to a bubbling spring, a *place of sunlight water* (its translated name), that proved dependable in a wilderness of sandstone.

Early automobile access was difficult, if not hazardous—six miles upstream through the mouth of the canyon; a trek that often required fighting a set of sand ruts going in and making your own coming out, and all the while keeping a wary eye for cloudbursts. In 1930, when trader Harry Rorick blasted a dugway up the east face so archaeologists and tourists could more easily reach the cliff dwelling of Betatakin seven miles

Shonto country.

away, it was described as the "roughest damn half-mile in America". It hasn't changed.

The post is in keeping with the people that it serves. The Navajos of the district have distinguished themselves for being the last stronghold of the "long hairs"—traditional clan groupings who hold fast to the old ways. Today, these proud ones are the descendants of those who made a fighting retreat into the recesses of Navajo Mountain and escaped the "Long Walk" and dregs of Bosque Redondo.

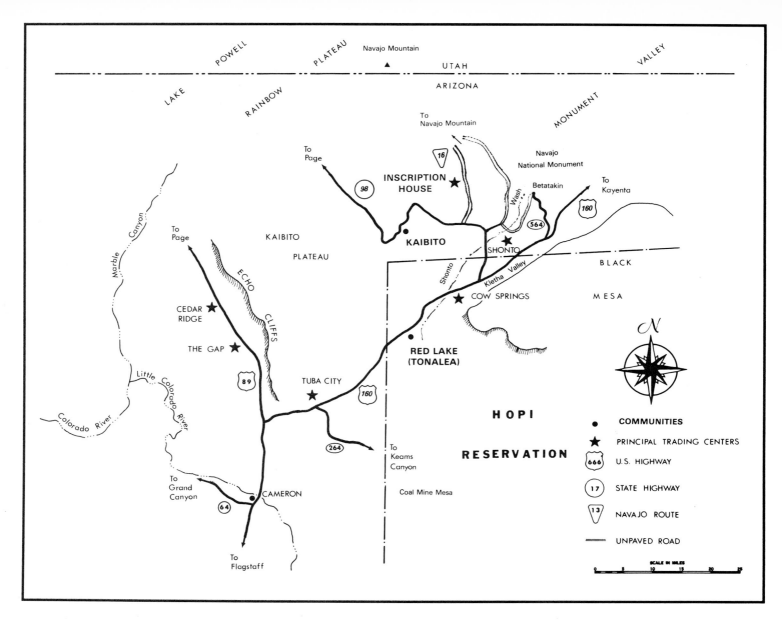

Western Reservation Area Map

20-Year Comparative Costs					Weavers
Year	**3 x 5**	**4 x 6**	**6 x 9**	**Large Specials**	Mary Begamble
					Lucille Begay
1968	$50-150	$200-300	$350-500	$650 & up	Helen Bigman
1978	$200-250	$300-400	$500-650	$1,000 & up	Veronica Begay
1988	$300-500	$500-750	$1,000-2,000	$3,000 & up	Lorinda Bennette

Trading Posts

Cedar Ridge Trading Post
Cow Springs Trading Post
Inscription House Trading Post
Shonto Trading Post
The Gap Trading Post
Tuba City Trading Post

Traders

Jerry Whiterock
Bennie Garcia
Al Townsend
Melissa and Ray Trolet
Jim Wilson
Jerry Norris

Weavers

Mary Begamble
Lucille Begay
Helen Bigman
Veronica Begay
Lorinda Bennette
Mary Clark
Mary Fowler
Anna Grayhat
Betty Ann Huskon
Leona Littleman
Mary S. Nez
Shirley Nockidench
  (Bird Rug weaver)
Bessie Sellers
Susie Tacheene
Mary Tisi
Lily Touchin
Lillie Nes Tsosi
Alice Williams

Chapter 14

SPECIALTY RUGS AND OTHER TYPES*

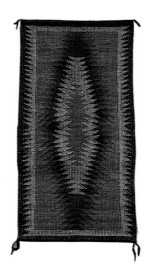

Monogram

Usually square and small in size, the Monogram Rug can carry almost any message the weaver desires; people's names, places of business, patriotic slogans, etc.

Outline

The Outline Rug features a multiple outlining of the designs in different colors. The rug is usually bordered encasing a large central motif, such as a diamond or square.

Raised Outline

More of a weaving technique than a style piece, the Raised Outline is basically an outline rug that employs an edging weft of a different color to be transported over two warps instead of the customary one. This produces an elevated design outline on one surface of the rug. *(See Chapter 12; also Additional Notes 55, 56.)*

---

*Because these rug types are woven throughout the reservation, no differentation is made as to preferences in wool/yarn usage, or dyes. It is inferred that a variety of methods and materials are utilized and employed in their construction.

Chief Blanket

Generally of small to moderate size, the modern-day Chief-designed rug is generally made of red, black, or dark-blue colored yarns, set in horizontal stripes interspaced with bands of white or gray. Smaller design elements, such as checks, diamonds and crosses, may occupy the center and corner edges. The rug has lost the significance for which it was named. (*See Additional Note 8.*) Its design continues to live, however, because of the historical prestige it once enjoyed.

Pictorial

Amsden (1934), in discussing Pictorial Rugs says: *It is doubtful if any weaver ever attempted to draw a picture to tell a story upon her loom until after the American conquest. Now she launches forth ambitiously with flags and rampant eagles and square-wheeled railway cars.*

As early as the late 1800s, Navajo weavers illustrated their textiles with pictures of animals and human forms. The Pictorial Rug of today is woven in a variety of usually bright colors. Likewise, a variety of subject matter is displayed depending upon the fancy of the weaver— pickup trucks, hogans, mountains, animals (particularly horses, cattle and sheep), and people are all portrayed, in a somewhat crowded manner.

Bird Rug

A type of a popular Pictorial Rug that has endured from early-day graphics to the present is a large, leafless tree with arrays of multiple-colored birds perched upon branches. The rug is generally small to moderate in size and usually without a border.

Monogram-Pictorial

Combining words with pictures on a rug is a relatively modern approach. An American flag with U.S.A. across the top, the name of a person, or the name of a trading post above a building all add personal touches to a rug that often conveys more meaning to whom it is directed, rather than general appeal.

Hide Rug

A rare specialty of moderate size that depicts the skinned rawhide of a cow. An imaginative piece that is woven to clearly outline the reddish-brown body (complete with tail) and white markings of a skinned hide. Some examples are expertly done and from distant viewing remarkably resembles a rawhide surface.

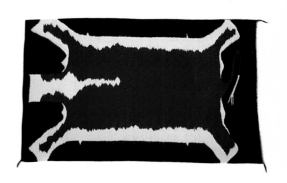

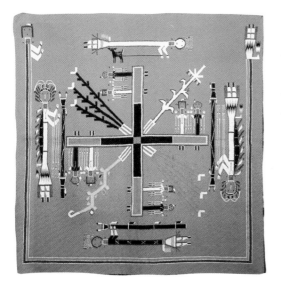

Circular Rug

Another innovation that has emerged is a small rug which surfaced in 1971. Completely circular (usually 18'' in circumference), it is woven in typical *Ganado* designs with red-black-gray-white colors. An air of intrigue surrounds the rug inasmuch as the weavers who accomplish this feat refuse to allow anyone to observe their technique or examine their loom. Some writers suspect a loom arrangement fashioned within the radius of a wagon wheel.

Sandpainting Rug

These rugs are woven copies, though not exact, of sandpainting designs. The rugs are light weight, unbordered, and square in size (3' x 3', 5' x 5'). Backgrounds are usually tan with brighter, multiple colors composing the designs. The overall depictions, taken from actual sacred healing designs, are quite busy and intricate. The favorite subjects in modern-day rugs are the sandpaintings of the Whirling Log, Shooting Chant, Water Creatures and the Earth Creatures.

Tufted Weave

An unusual rug not too often found in contemporary weaving is the tufted weave— the second front and back side in a Navajo fabric. In essence, it is a shag-type rug accomplished by inserting long strands of Angora goat wool in the weft threads. It is of small and irregular size and shape. In some instances, weavers use the piece as a cushion surface during weaving.

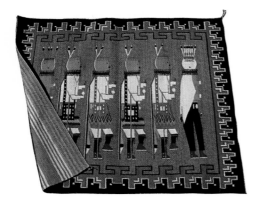

Two-Faced Rug

A difficult rug, the Two-Faced is actually a fabric in which the two sides display entirely different designs and colors. To achieve this, the weaver places the weft threads one behind the other, instead of the conventional placement with threads placed atop one another. The rug is rare and understandably expensive. Being doubled in thickness in a two-styles-in-one development, it is more often coarse-textured and heavy. The Two-Faced Rug dates from the late 1880s. It has never been extremely popular, but because of its unique and novel construction, it is attractive for collectors.

Twills

The term "twill" not only signifies a rug type, but also a style of weaving that is achieved through arrangement of the loom heddles. Amsden (1934) explains: *Twilling is a constant diagonal progression of stitches produced by the regular alteration of the point of insertion of warp and weft. The plain weave, for example, uses but two sheds, permitting no alteration of this point; the result is a fabric of vertical ribs with one string of warp (commonly) as the core of each. Twilling on the other hand (as done by the Navajo), employs four sheds, controlled by three heddles and the shed rod, the heddle arrangement being calculated to throw each stitch of weft one warp string to the right or left of the one preceding it. The result is a fabric of diagonal rather than vertical ribs.*

All twill weaves are constructed by carrying the weft over more than one warp at a time, thus adding thickness (bulk) throughout the entire fabric. Twill-constructed rugs, because of the heavier texture, are popular and more suited as floor coverings and saddle blankets.

Basically there are three types of twill design: (1) diamond twill, (2) braided (herringbone or diagonal), and (3) plain twill.

Diamond Twill

Braided Twill

Double Weave

The term "double weave" is a twill variation combining a braided twill alternated with a diamond twill that has the order of colors reversed on the two sides. The pattern remains identical, but by alternating colors through the entire width of the sheds, the arrangement of color changes from one side to the other, but maintains the same mirrored position.

Saddle Blanket

The Saddle Blanket is the only Navajo textile woven today that the Indians use for a functional purpose. It comes in two sizes: single (30″ x 30″) and double (30″ x 60″). The blanket is purposely coarse-woven to take hard wear beneath the saddle. The format is usually unbordered, featuring simple serration and stripe and band designs. Colors are mostly bright, particularly at the corners and ends. Tassels are sometimes incorporated at the four corners in the more elaborate pieces. Twill weaving is used quite often in developing the piece. Many people use the Saddle Blanket as a floor item, mainly because of its durability.

Single

Double

Four-In-One

Perhaps the rarest rug in comtemporary Navajo weaving is the Four-In-One style. It consists of four equal quadrants enclosed in a bordered format. Each square contains a separate design, each different from the other three. Some Four-In-One rugs display pairs of squares, i.e. two Sandpaintings and two Pictorials.

These rugs require a great deal of imagination, talent and perseverance. They are rarely attempted and are highly prized.

Gallup Throw

Referred to by some writers as a regional style rug, the Gallup Throw is actually a tourist curio item developed near Gallup during the 1930s for railroad passengers. Today it can be found woven in many places on the reservation.

Some novice weavers practice with the throw-type rug before attempting more difficult designs and weaves. It is a small, inexpensive, borderless runner or table-top piece, often possessing a cotton warp, which is usually left dangling as a one or two-inch fringe at the ends. The rug is commonly of bright colors. Designs are relatively simple; broad chevrons, stripes, stylized diamonds, and some displaying the Yei figure.

Other Types

Woman's Dress

This fabric is not a rug, but represents still another example of a Navajo woven product. The style of the Woman's Dress dates from the earliest influences of Pueblo women on the Navajo mode of attire. Design of the Navajo Woman's Dress is different from the plain Pueblo style, in that the Puebloans utilized one piece that was of sufficient width to permit doubling. The Navajo Woman's Dress consists of two pieces of identical size and shape to be worn as front and back pieces. It is secured at the top and bottom, with long slits prevailing on the sides to allow for arm movement. There are no sleeves. Simple stripes and small design elements decorate the piece in synthetic colors of black, red, and blue.

The piece still retains the basic early style and design of centuries. Three large panels, with alternating blocks of color, comprise the overall presentation, with interspacings of smaller stripes and bands. Small geometrics, such as rows of diamonds or checks, usually decorate the top and bottom sections.

A smaller version of the Woman's Dress, appropriately called Child's Dress, occasionally finds its way into rug outlets. These are quite rare and are sought as collectors' items.

Cross

This fabric, though actually not a rug (in the truest sense), is more of a symbol of the Late Classic Period Moqui (Hopi) cross that Hubbell popularized in his *Ganado* motifs. Not only depicted as a cross, but also woven in the cross shape, it is quite unusual and appeals particularly to the serious collector. Usually attempted in moderate sizes (2' x 2'), it is utilized mostly as a table-top feature, or as a striking wall hanging.

Miniatures

Gaining popularity as collector items, miniature weavings are quite unique in reduced replicas of the standard creation. They represent all of the regional styles (plus some specialties), and are constructed with a variety of natural wool, processed wool and commercial yarn, and utilize both synthetic and vegetal dyes. In the good to outstanding examples, the smaller the size (involving finer stitching), the higher the price—being regarded as diminutive pieces of fine art. They range in size from a postage stamp to several inches square. The Fort Defiance area is noted for miniature weavings.

Standard Loom

A major woven product that is entact on a traditional log-constructed loom. These dominant examples are rare and most are special ordered for specific purposes, i.e., exhibits in museums and visitor's centers.

Miniature Loom

A popular novelty item, but very representative of an actual miniature rug woven on an actual miniature loom. Some come completely equipped with a spindle, fork, batten, tow cards, and shed and heddle rods. Most models stand 12'' high and feature a variety of designs and dyes. The looms are very effective in publicizing Navajo weaving, and particularly in an educational sense, because the majority of non-Indians seldom witness the physical presence of a rug on a loom. In home decorating they pose an attractive visual display as mantle pieces.

Pillow-Top Covers

These woven covers add a distinction in contemporary home decorating. Their usage is somewhat limited, however, and are not always available, because it involves an off-reservation source for pillow manufacturing. Colors lack a broad range, leaning more toward the pastel shades to satisfy home schemes. Designs are likewise simple and do not represent any regional style, but instead display uncomplicated patterns. Some Yei-designed pillow tops found in the Shiprock area are well done and present more of a traditional Navajo image.

General Rug

A fabric of almost any dimension, poor to excellent weave, featuring handspun, processed or commercial yarn, synthetic or vegetal-dyed, incorporating a multitude of designs, bordered or borderless. It may be woven in any locale on the reservation. The distinction of the general rug is that it does not possess sufficient characteristics to warrant recognition as a regional style rug or a specialty rug. The majority of rugs woven on the reservation today (40%) are in this category.

Special-Order Rug

Maxwell (1963) may have been a perfectionist when he suggested that anybody requiring a made-to-order rug should either learn to weave or marry a weaver! True, a definite communication problem exists between weaver and customer. What may start out to be an understanding of size, color, dye and style invariably changes as the rug develops. Some weavers still sell their craft through their area trader, and, understandably so, is the only non-Indian who can suggest, influence, or commission for a certain type of rug. The price for special-order rugs is usually quite high and the results almost always uncertain. Acquaintances made with traders and weavers on the reservation, however, can sometimes result in getting just what you ordered (**Plate 9**).

Additional Notes

Chapter 1
History

The People

1. With the transfer of the Navajos back to their homeland, it was felt that Fort Wingate was too far removed from areas of resettlement to adequately assist in their supervision. General Getty explored the possibility of reestablishing the garrison further to the west. Fort Canby, which was abandoned after the "Navajo roundup" (October 8, 1864), would have been the ideal relocation site. The post, however, was in a state of complete ruin. Furthermore, being located 35 miles north of the main east-west road, it would have been economically unfeasible for the distribution of supplies and equipment. Getty decided, therefore, that the administration point would be established at Bear Springs, and subsequently ordered the reactivation of Fort Lyon (old Fort Fauntleroy), but calling it the "new" Fort Wingate (James, 1967).

    As unforeseen by the government, the tendency for the displacees to gravitate toward the core of their *Dineth* (northwest to Canyon de Chelly), the further the distance became for the distribution of supplies from Fort Wingate. In the summer of 1868, the Bureau of Indian Affairs, under the guardianship of an agent, transferred their office to the ramshackled Fort Canby and restored its former name—Fort Defiance. The military, in a gesture of passive presence, remained at Fort Wingate.

The Traders

2. McNitt (1962, p.47n) reports that a few nomadic-type traders were licensed to patronize the Navajos in the early 1850s. Auguste LaCome, of French extraction, was granted a license in January 1853—thus, being the earliest recorded Navajo trader.

3. Piñon, Spanish for "pine kernel" (called *neschi* by the Navajos), is an edible nut about the size of a small pea. It occurs in the cones of the brushy Piñon Pine (*Pinus edulis*) at elevations of 6,000-8,000 feet. Along the reaches of the Chuska Mountains and Defiance Plateau on the east, and in western sectors of the Shonto high country, the piñon forests are thick, although bountiful crops only develop every 3-5 years. Those trading posts that were situated near these forested environs usually did a considerable business with this additional commodity. Harvested in the fall, the nuts were sacked in 90-pound bags and wholesaled out of Gallup, New Mexico, to be shipped to populous markets where they were cleaned, processed (salted), packaged and sold similar to peanuts. The *McKinley County Republican* reported on November 24, 1911, that one local wholesaler alone had contracted for 60,000 pounds of nuts, at five cents a pound. Kluckhohn and Leighton (1946) stated that one trader in 1936 paid out $18,000 in piñon nuts.

4. Early trade was without monetary exchange. A simple hands across the counter transaction prevailed—a good rug for some canned goods, an enamel bucket and three yards of velveteen; or, six sheep for a saddle, an axe and a black, wide-rimmed Mallory hat. As refinements in purchases were introduced, tokens (called *secos*) were used as legal tender. Usually made of a brass alloy (some were leather), these chips were issued in

various denominations and were often stamped with the trader's name, implying their value was only redeemable at his post. *Secos* were discontinued in 1935.

5. Even in the modern era, the trader is not allowed to own the land that his post is situated upon. The arrangement with the Navajo Tribe is a periodic lease renewal policy, and if the trader decides to vacate, or the lease is revoked, the investment of buildings and inventory can only be sold to another trader. After World War II, the Tribe instituted a proceeds lease arrangement, whereby the trader is taxed on a percentage of his monthly sales.

6. The hogan (*hoghan*) is the basic Navajo dwelling. Contructed of variable conbinations of logs, brush, mud and rock, the unit can be one of two forms—conical or the six-sided dome shape. Guest hogans at trading posts began to appear around the turn of the century. They were primarily erected to accomodate those Indians who had to travel a great distance to trade, or who were stranded by bad weather. At Shonto, four guest hogans were built in 1930 in hopes of enticing tourists to "lay over" during their tours of the Indian country. (*See title page sketch.*) These shelters may have been the primitive prototype of the modern-day motel. An interesting side feature to the Shonto hogans were their use in a 1932 Universal Pictures movie entitled *Laughing Boy*. This on-location motion picture was undoubtedly the first filmed on the reservation and preceded the classic (John Ford) Western, *Stagecoach*, filmed in nearby Monument Valley, by six years.

The Craft

7. Foote and Schackel (1986, p.21) report that Pueblo men of this period were the principal weavers in the household.

8. The Chief Blanket is somewhat controversial. Some writers have clouded its origin and intent by stating that Navajos did not have chiefs, and that the blanket was woven principally as a highly prized barter item for chiefs of other Indian tribes; hence its name. This is erroneous. The fact remains that the Navajos did recognize chiefs and that various headsmen are shown in photographs adorned with the fabric. It was not, however, a symbol of rank or leadership and anyone could wear them. Because the blanket represented a superior weave and possessed design appeal, it became an expensive item to own, and was usually only affordable by the more influencial and wealthy—"the chiefs" (Martin Link, personal communication, 1988). The chief pattern evolved through four recognized phases of development depending upon the variable uses of dyes and patterns (Houlihan and others, 1987, p.53; Kaufman and Selser, 1985, p. 27-33).

9. Navajo weavers had access to bayeta early in the 1800s, but only in rare quantity. Amsden (1934, p. 142n) refers to the first half of the 19th century as the "bayeta period". The natural source of the color red used in bayeta was from dyes called lac and cochineal, which were produced from the powdered remains of Mexican cactus beetles.

10. The period between 1880-1890 became known as the era of the "eye-dazzlers". With the analine-dyed Germantown yarns to work with, the weavers now possessed a full spectrum of vibrant colors. The designs remained basically Mexican-Saltillo diamond motifs, which consisted of multiple outlines and zigzags that often resulted in an explosion of combating colors. Many examples were woven with decorative fringe threads at the top and bottom. Today, the "eyedazzler" is much in demand as a collector item.

11. James (1934) credits a Fort Defiance trader named Ben Hyatt with introducing aniline dyes to the reservation in 1878. The term "aniline", which denotes a coal-tar based colorant, was the prominent early synthetic dye in common use on the reservation during the last decades of the 19th century.

12. The concept of the bordered rug may have been introduced to weavers as early as the Bosque Redondo days. During their confinement, the Navajos were supplied with thousands of Hispanic-woven (Rio Grande) blankets for wearing apparel. These items included modifications of old Mexican-Saltillo designs, some of which may have included borders (Kaufman and Selser, 1985, p.53). Amsden (1934, p.170) states that the first bordered rug dates from 1873.

13. The teaming of Hubbell and the Fred Harvey Company proved to be a lucrative association, and by the turn of the century, Hubbell undoubtedly was one of the leading rug dealers in America. In the year 1902 alone, Hubbell, negotiating through Harvey's representative buyer, Herman Schweizer, sold $60,000 worth of rugs (Kaufman and Selser, 1985).

14. Moore also experimented with machine-spun wool and commercially dyed yarns (Bulow, 1986).

15. Two areas in the regional style are currently breaking down. The *Chinle* rug is losing its identity because of a lack of trader stimuli, and also because its distinguishing characteristics are being absorbed by more popular styles (i.e., *Crystal, Wide Ruins*). Similarly, the area denoted as Western Reservation, generally accepted as the birthplace of the Storm Pattern rug, is no longer the dominant weaving center for this style piece. In a counter move, a vegetal-dyed (commercial yarn), raised outline-style rug with *Teec Nos Pos* designs (called the *New Lands*), is slowly gaining popularity as a new regional style (*see Chapter 12*).

16. Some clarification is necessary on the definition of processed wool and commercial yarn, as both terms are being bantered about almost interchangeably. Processed wool, or "roving", as it is sometimes called, is raw wool that has been plant cleaned and carded into grades of undyed fibers that is packaged into 25-pound bales. Weavers can purchase the wool in varying quantities, spin it, and either vegetal or synthetic dye the product to their liking.

   Commercial yarn is already processed wool that has been spun into various ply grades (usually in one-ply skeins). In most instances, it has already been synthetically dyed, either in bright colors or soft pastel hues that resemble the vegetal tones, or uncolored skeins can be vegetal dyed with traditional plant recipes. In some instances, a weaver will purchase lighter shades of colored yarn and overdye it with a concoction of her own to create an entirely new tone. Because commercial yarns are already spun, ply measured and obtainable in a multiple range of colors, it is this time-saving product that is in principal use in the craft today.

17. Because of the higher prices being commanded (and received) by weavers, many are returning to the loom, including some elderly women. Children are also being trained at an early age, and teenaged weavers in some locales are turning out excellent pieces. Several traders also report that men are beginning to submit rugs for sale. Bruce Burnham (personal communication, 1987) of Sanders, Arizona, suspects that from the good to excellent products that he has seen recently, that some men may have been "closet weavers" for a number of years, but sold their products under their wife's name because it wasn't a manly activity. Now that the craft is economically attractive and has been elevated to a true art form,

this is no longer the situation. Burnham reports, that the best-of-show weavers have recently been men, and in producing the raised outline textile (in the Sanders area), outnumber the women.

18. Some traders refer uncomplimentary to this practice as "hogan-hopping".

Chapter 2
From Sheep To Rug

19. Reference to the color black as a natural wool tone is a misnomer. In most cases it is dyed synthetically to further intensify its balance, because natural shorn black wool is not a deep solid black.

20. The preparation of the warp thread is done during the spinning process. In almost all cases the threads are natural wool—the one exception being the prevalent use of cotton warp in the small table-top covers of the *Gallup Throw*.

21. Amsden (1934) outlined nine types of Navajo weaves, they are: Plain weave, double weave, two-faced weave, and six twill weaves. The tapestry technique is employed in all of these types. It is the arrangement of the heddles that produces the variants. The so-called "wedge weave" might be considered the one exception, whereby the basic horizontal attitude of the warp is altered. Though rarely practiced in modern time, the "wedge weave" (called "pulled warp" by Amsden), enjoyed popularity during the 1880s-1890s. The principal approach was the stretching of the warp at oblique angles to allow the weft to conform to desired patterns, which were usually set in diagonal, interlocking zigzags. Some writings referred to this style as "lighting weave".

22. Considering those fabrics that are well woven, the finely constructed commercial yarns are running from $150-$200 a square foot; vegetal dyes $200-$250 a square foot; and the natural wool products upwards of $300 a square foot.

23. One of the more interesting facets of the trading post system that has gone unreported, is that traders often trade among themselves. This has added significantly to the circulation of rug styles throughout the reservation.

Chapter 3
Shiprock

24. Also located within the Shiprock weaving area, particularly around the trading posts of Cove and Red Rock, are weavers who produce excellent Sandpainting rugs.

Chapter 5
Teec Nos Pos

25. Black Horse (*Be-sho-she*), a Beautiful Mountain area clan chieftan, whose dislike for the white man prompted defiant behavior, was responsible for a near rebellion in 1913 that neccesitated quelling by U.S. Army troops from Fort Bliss, Texas (McKibben, 1954). The incident which spawned the uprising was the arrest of several clan members involved in plural marriages.

Chapter 6
Crystal

26. Simpson (1850, p.78)

27. Also referred to as Cottonwood Pass. Post Office discontinued in 1914. Mail service now directed through Navajo, New Mexico.

28. Record Group #75, No. 11520 (1884). National Archives, Washington, D.C.

29. When Charlie Newcomb first began trading at Crystal in 1922, a considerable amount of "Moore wool" was still on hand. It was Newcomb's supposition that the machine-processed fiber was milled somewhere in Wisconsin (McNitt, 1962, p.254n).

Assisted by his wife, Moore also experimented with synthetic dyes, and reportedly they spent long hours in their kitchen preparing dyed wool for area weavers. Don Jensen transmitted to the author (written communication, February 3, 1975) that shortly after he purchased the post, Moore's daughter paid a visit to Crystal. It was her recounting that her parents passed away prematurely in Kansas in 1923 from what she attributed to "lead poisoning" from prolonged inhaling of dyebath fumes in galvanized pails.

30. Moore's sudden departure from Crystal was clouded with controversy. A local welfare scandal involving heating oil supplies, in which he was not personally involved, was embarrassing to the point of forcing his leave.

31. Don Jensen, who traded at Crystal between 1944 and 1981, is responsible for the development of the modern *Crystal* rug. Jensen credits a frequent visitor, a Dr. Hunt, professor at Stanford University and part-time collector and buyer for *Sunset Magazine*, for encouraging a return to Classic Period stripes and bands constructed with vegetal dyes on a borderless format. His clue (Hunts') being the earlier successes at Chinle and Wide Ruins in the adoption of this style. Jensen further elaborates that there was some minor vegetal dyeing being attempted in the area a few years prior to his residency, and that a weaver named Des-bah-Nez is credited with being the first Crystal weaver to utilize plant concoctions in wool colors.

32. The "wavy-line" technique is a distinct *Crystal* trait and creation. Don Jensen reports that the first rug he saw with this undulating feature was by Imelda Nez in 1944. Jensen says that the technique caught on quickly, but that its ultimate popularity prompted weavers to ask a higher price for rugs that incorporated the feature.

Chapter 7
Two Gray Hills

33. Post Office was called Crozier. Mail service was discontinued in 1919 and transferred to Newcomb, New Mexico. In recent years trading residents have received their mail through Tohatchi, New Mexico.

34. Carded black and white = gray; carded brown and white = tan and beige.

Chapter 8
Chinle

35. Spelled Chin Lee prior to 1941, and at times, Chinlee. It roughly translates to, "it flows from the canyon".

36. This site later served as the location for the first Post Office building in Chinle. The hillock is situated directly across the main road (north) from the Catholic Church.

37. Sam Day is credited with the discovery of Massacre Cave and other significant archaeological findings in Canyon de Chelly in 1904. His son, Charles, was later appointed the first custodian (pre-National Park Service management) in protecting artifacts of the canyon. Day, who led a varied and colorful life, was already of advanced age when licensed to trade. He was a lanky six-footer who was born in Canton, Ohio, in 1845. A drifter of sorts, he had briefly studied civil engineering in Newark, New Jersey, before joining the Union Army during the Civil War. After his enlistment, he headed west to the gold fields of South Dakota, found a young woman (Anna P. Burnbridge, who married him in Iowa), and eventually settled in Colorado for a short time. Hired as a surveyor for the federal government, Day and his family found themselves in Arizona in the early 1880s where he homesteaded and worked for several years delineating the eastern and southern boundaries of the Navajo Reservation (Harrison and Spears, 1987).

Following his trading days at Chinle, Day retired to his homestead at Cienega Amarilla, Spanish for "yellow marsh". He had established the property prior to its inclusion within the boundaries of the reservation. In later years he donated the land to the Franciscan O.F.M. Order for use as a hospital and school for Indian children; it was renamed St. Michaels. Located a short distance west of present-day Window Rock, Arizona, the place is now a designated historic site.

38. Bostonian reared, Mary Cabot Wheelwright was a scholar of world comparative religions. She arrived in the Southwest in 1918 and became enamored with Navajo traditions.She established a friendship with the famous medicine man, Hosteen Klah of Newcomb, New Mexico, and together in 1937 they founded the House of Navajo Religion in Santa Fe. It later evolved to become the Wheelwright Museum of the American Indian. Miss Wheelwright died in 1948.

Chapter 9
Ganado

39. The Crary site, the first trading post after Fort Defiance, is thought to have been located on Pueblo Colorado Wash near Ganado Lake, three miles northeast of the present Hubbell post. The Leonard location, in all probability, is the original ground of Hubbell's later operation.

McNitt (1962, p.201n) points out some discrepancies in the chronology of events that established the Hubbell post. Late in life, Hubbell (1930) states that he purchased his holdings in 1876 from a man named "Williams." In the National Archives (Record Group #75), records show that Lorenzo was still employed as a clerk at Fort Defiance during the summer and fall of 1876, and it seems unlikely that his trading days could have started at that time. The "Williams" that Hubbell was referring to may have been Perry H. Williams, who on March 31, 1877, was licensed to trade at Washington Pass. It could also have been George M. "Barney" Williams, who was mentioned by Bourke (1884) as trading on Pueblo Colorado Wash in 1881. [This "Williams" more than likely operated at the old Crary location.]

Four years after Lorenzo's death, Eckel (1934) wrote that the founding sequence of Hubbell Trading Post started with Charles Crary who sold to Leonard in 1875, who in turn, sold to Hubbell the following year (1876). Since Eckel was Hubbell's granddaughter, many historians have accepted her writings as fact. From the documented presence of Leonard during 1876-78, however, logical assumption is to place Hubbell at Ganado in late 1876, possibly clerking for Leonard, then buying him out in 1878. Hubbell later applied for and was granted a homestead of 160 acres at the site. This was before the area was included within the expanded boundaries of the reservation in 1880.

40. Hubbell was born in 1853 at Pajarito, New Mexico, the son of a Connecticut Yankee who had gone to New Mexico as a soldier and married into a family of Spanish descent. Mostly self-educated, he became familiar with the life, ways and language of the Navajos while traveling about the Southwest as a young man and serving as a clerk and a Spanish interpreter.

Hubbell—"Old Mexican" or "Double Glasses" to the Navajos, was not only their merchant, but also their guide and teacher in understanding the ways of the white man. He was the trusted friend who translated and wrote letters, settled family quarrels, explained Government policy, and helped the sick.

When a smallpox epidemic swept the reservation in 1886, he worked night and day caring for the sick and dying, using his own home as a hospital. He was immune because of a boyhood bout with the disease, but the Navajos ascribed it to a higher power.

Hubbell had an enduring influence on Navajo rug weaving and silversmithing, for he consistently demanded and promoted excellence in craftsmanship. He built a trading empire that included stage and freight lines, as well as several trading posts. At various times, he and his two sons, together or separately, owned 24 trading posts, a wholesale house in Winslow, and other business and ranch properties. Beyond question, he was the foremost Navajo trader of his time.

Hubbell actively participated in politics. His career inspired novels and other literature, including a short story by Hamlin Garland about his service as sheriff of Apache County in the 1880s. He served in the Territorial Council, helped guide Arizona to statehood, was a State Senator, and ran unsuccessfully for the U.S. Senate.

Hubbell's political philosophy was quite liberal for his time. He was a supporter of women's rights to vote, opposed to disenfranchising the Spanish-speaking Americans through use of literary requirements in English, and favored prohibition. He conducted himself so honorably in his campaigns for office that even his opponents complimented him on his methods. He did not lack conviction, however, and was noted for his tenacity and enthusiasm in debate.

When he was first elected sheriff, Texas cattlemen invaded the sheep country of Apache County. Hubbell backed the sheepmen. Recollecting the bloody conflict he said, *I'd been shot at from ambush no less than a dozen times, and my home had been converted into a veritable fort. For one solid year not a member of my family went to bed except behind doors and windows barricaded with mattresses or sand bags.*

Though he had political inclinations, he was always primarily a businessman. One admirer wrote. . . *it was because he was just and honest and humane that he held this unquestioned supremacy among traders with the Navajos.* Hubbell expressed his business philosophy this way: *The first duty of an Indian trader, in my belief, is to look after the material welfare of his neighbors; to advise them to produce that which their natural inclinations and talent best adapts them; to treat them honestly and insist upon getting the same treatment from them...to find a market for their products and vigilantly watch that they keep improving in the production of same, and advise them which commands the best price. This does not mean that the trader should forget that he is to see that he makes a fair profit for himself, for whatever would injure him would naturally injure those with whom he comes in contact.*

Hubbell's career as a trader spanned critical years for the Navajos. He came to the reservation when they were grasping for an adjustment to reservation life, with the ordeal of the "Long Walk," including confinement at Fort Sumner, New Mexico, fresh in their minds. More than any other white man, he helped them find that adjustment. He was often their spokesman and contact with the outside world. Though a Roman Catholic, Hubbell persuaded the Presbyterian Board of Foreign Missions to choose nearby Ganado for a mission site and, while the mission was being built, took the first missionaries into his home for a year.

He died on November 12, 1930, and was buried on Hubbell Hill, overlooking the trading post. One old man expressed the sadness of his fellow Navajos when he said:

You wear out your shoes, you buy another pair;
When the food is all gone, you buy more;
You gather melons, and more will grow on the vine;
You grind your corn and make bread which you eat;
And next year you have plenty more corn;
But my friend Don Lorenzo is gone, and none to take his place.
—Courtesy: National Park Service, 1986.

41. The succession of traders, following Southwest Parks And Monuments Association management, include: Bill Young (1967-1979), Al Grieves (1979-1982), and Bill Malone (1982-present).

Chapter 10
Wide Ruins

42. Following John Rieffer's death, the Wide Ruins post was closed in 1982. The store later burned and the remaining complex has now been razed.

43. Prior to 1880, the Wide Ruins area was not part of the Navajo Reservation, therefore, early merchants (not requiring licenses) cannot be traced through government records.

44. Subsequent excavations by the National Geographic Society dates the erection of Kinteel sometime between 1265-1285 A.D.

45. Sallie (Lippincott) Wagner reported to the author that during their stay in California they sold out to a man named Carl Hine, in 1942, but reacquired the property two years later by repossession.

46. Sallie (Lippincott) Wagner reported that when they began trading at Wide Ruins in 1938 the weaving effort was in a terrible state. The main products were gaudy, poorly woven pillow top covers that were sold in curio stands along old U.S. 66.

47. In some rug descriptions, the term "Lippincott pink" is occasionally used to describe a particular hue attributed to a *Wide Ruins* product that Sallie (Lippincott) Wagner says was obtained from the red lichen that grew on oak trees.

Chapter 11
Burntwater

48. The Burnt Water (spelled Burntwater in the rug type) Trading Post was closed in 1983.

49. Jacobs also credits Laura Murphy, another expert area weaver, with early contributions to the *Burntwater* rug.

50. Bruce Burnham is initiating experiments by issuing uncolored commercial yarn to area weavers to be native plant dyed with home recipes.

Chapter 12
Western Reservation

51. The Red Lake Trading Post was closed in the spring of 1987 and a new "general" (convenience) store, no longer in the trading business, is located one-half mile to the west.

52. Letter communication: Paul Babbitt, Jr., Babbitt Brothers Trading Company, Flagstaff, Arizona (November 23, 1973).

53. The Western Reservation is also noted for two speciality type weaves: Pictorals (particularly Bird Rugs) are in evidence around The Gap trading area and Shonto is known for its Saddle Blankets.

54. The four sacred mountains of Navajo mythology are: East—*Sisnaajini* (Sierra Blanca, Colorado); West—*Doko'ooaliid* (San Francisco Peak, Arizona); North—*Dibentsaa* (Mount Hesperus, Colorado); and South—*Tsoodzil* (Mount Taylor, New Mexico.

Chapter 13
New Lands

55. The raised outline weave is referred to by weavers as *Hoshtodi,* which translates in visual meaning to the variegated feathers of the Bull Bat Owl.

    Kent (1981, p.20) questions the time and origin of the raised outline technique that is attributed to Ned Hatathi and the Coal Mine Mesa weavers in 1950. She cites a raised outline textile, now in collection at the Museum of Northern Arizona, in Flagstaff, which was woven at Ganado in 1934. This evidence predates the guild project by sixteen years.

56. Kent (1981, p.20) describes the raised outline technique as... *basically a plain weave tapestry, but along the edges of two figures, where wefts meet and turn back on themselves, there appears to be a ridge. This is what gives the weave its name. The effect is obtained by inserting a weft of one color, followed by a weft of another color in the next shed. Both wefts move in the same direction—say from right to left. When they reach the edge of the figure they are making, each passes over two warps, instead of the usual one. It is these long floats that appear to be raised.*

57. Between 1878 and 1886 the Navajo Reservation was enlarged by five land additions. One of these, the Navajo-Hopi Joint Use Area, was created by an Executive Order signed by President Chester A. Arthur on December 16, 1882. This action, which has plagued northern Arizona for over a century, carved out two and a half million acres (for sharing with the Navajo) from what the Hopi Tribe believed to be their traditional land. In subsequent years, a clash of cultures and wills prevailed over the land sharing, resulting in some violence, numerous court actions and federal suits. A bitter resolve culminated in 1974 when the U.S. Congress voted 90,000 acres of disputed land to be turned back exclusively to the Hopis. A Navajo-Hopi Joint Land Commission was ultimately created to oversee and manage a peaceful transition. Over 1,200 Navajo families have now been relocated from the contested area; more are destined to follow. Iverson (1988) points out that the dispute in land occupancy is an equitable situation, and that Hopis, although smaller in numbers, who are residing on Navajo property, are also subject to relocation.

58. Bruce Burnham (personal communication, 1988) reported that the land acquisition was in excess of one million acres centered approximately 15 miles southeast of Sanders. Some residences have already been constructed, and a New Lands Chapter is planned for the near future.

Plate Descriptions

Front Cover
Ganado (37" X 63")
Weaver: Evelyn Curley
Source: Hubbell Trading Post, Ganado, AZ (1987)
Construction: Mostly synthetic dyed, processed white, natural carded gray, all handspun.

Frontispiece
Monogram Pictoral (15" X 16")
Weaver: Unknown
Source: Author's collection (1981)
Construction: Synthetic-dyed figures and designs, some minor commercial yarn in outlines, natural carded gray, mostly handspun.

Plate 1
Shiprock Yei (27" X 41")
Weaver: Bernia Pettygras, Shiprock, NM
Source: Author's collection (1969)
Construction: Mostly synthetic dyed, some minor commercial yarn in outlines, processed white, natural carded gray, mostly handspun.

Plate 2
Shiprock Yei (40" X 40")
Weaver: Unknown
Source: Courtesy, Covered Wagon, Albuquerque, NM (1970)
Construction: Synthetic-dyed figures and designs, processed white background, minor commercial yarn, mostly handspun.

Plate 3
Shiprock Yeibechai (30" X 36")
Weaver: Rose Peshlakai, Shiprock, NM
Source: Private collection (1970)
Construction: Synthetic dyed, processed white, all handspun.

Plate 4
Lukachukai Yei (36" X 60")
Weaver: Unknown
Source: Courtesy, Hubbell Trading Post, Ganado, AZ (1968)
Construction: Partly synthetic dyed, natural white, natural carded gray, some vegetal dyes, all handspun.

Plate 5
Lukachukai Yei (40" X 40")
Weaver: Unknown
Source: Courtesy, Hubbell Trading Post, Ganado, AZ (1968)
Construction: Partly synthetic dyed, natural white, some vegetal dyes, all handspun.

Plate 6
Teec Nos Pos (72" X 108")
Weaver: Unknown
Source: Courtesy, Covered Wagon, Albuquerque, NM (1970)
Construction: Synthetic dyed, processed white, all handspun.

Plate 7
Teec Nos Pos (31" X 44")
Weaver: Unknown
Source: Courtesy, Covered Wagon, Albuquerque, NM (1970)
Construction: Synthetic dyed, processed white, all handspun.

Plate 8
Teec Nos Pos (48" X 72")
Weaver: Louise Cattleman, Teec Nos Pos, AZ
Source: Private collection (1969)
Construction: Partly synthetic dyed, partly vegetal dyed, natural white, some minor commercial yarn, mostly handspun.

Plate 9
Crystal (36" X 60")
Weaver: Mary Moore, Crystal, NM
Source: Author's collection (1969)
Construction: All vegetal dyed, all handspun.
Remarks: Special-order rug incorporating Greek frets of early John B. Moore design into contemporary horizontal banded format.

Plate 10
Crystal (36" X 60")
Weaver: Elsie Yazzie, Window Rock, AZ
Source: Private collection (1973)
Construction: Partly vegetal dyed, natural carded gray, processed white, all handspun.

Plate 11
Crystal Type (38" X 48")
Weaver: Unknown
Source: Author's collection (1969)
Construction: Mostly vegetal dyed, natural carded gray, synthetic-dyed red, all handspun.

Plate 12
Crystal (39½" X 59½")
Weaver: Mary Alexander, Crystal, NM
Source: Bleser/Stabel collection, Tumacacori, AZ (1970)
Construction: Partly vegetal dyed, natural carded gray, all handspun.

Plate 13
Crystal (32" X 42")
Weaver: Lydia Peshlakai, Crystal, NM
Source: Author's collection (1987)
Construction: All vegetal dyed, all handspun.

Plate 14
Two Gray Hills Tapestry (30" X 46")
Weaver: Unknown
Source: Courtesy, Price's All Indian Shop, Albuquerque, NM (1970)
Construction: Synthetic black, natural wool carded blends, all handspun.

Plate 15
Two Gray Hills Tapestry (32" X 48")
Weaver: Unknown
Source: Courtesy, Price's All Indian Shop, Albuquerque, NM (1970)
Construction: Synthetic black, natural wool carded blends, all handspun.

Plate 16
Two Gray Hills Tapestry (32" X 40")
Weaver: Unknown
Source: Courtesy, Price's All Indian Shop, Albuquerque, NM (1970)
Construction: Synthetic black, natural wool carded blends, all handspun.

Plate 17
Two Gray Hills Tapestry (24" X 36")
Weaver: Unknown
Source: Courtesy, Price's All Indian Shop, Albuquerque, NM (1970)
Construction: Synthetic black, natural wool carded blends, all handspun.

Plate 18
Two Gray Hills Tapestry (24" X 36")
Weaver: Unknown
Source: Courtesy, Price's All Indian Shop, Albuquerque, NM (1970)
Construction: Synthetic black, natural wool carded blends, all handspun.

Plate 19
Two Gray Hills (33½" X 52½")
Weaver: Mary Bainbridge, Toadlena, NM
Source: Private collection (1970)
Construction: Synthetic black, natural wool carded blends, all handspun.

Plate 20
Chinle (36" X 44")
Weaver: Unknown
Source: Courtesy, Hubbell Trading Post, Ganado, AZ (1970)
Construction: Partly synthetic dyed, partly vegetal dyed, all handspun.

Plate 21
Chinle Rugs (32" X 46")
Weaver: Ella Yazzie, Chinle, AZ
Source: Courtesy, Thunderbird Lodge, Chinle, AZ (1987)
Construction: All commercial yarn.

Plate 22
Chinle (34" X 48")
Weaver: Nes Bah Lee, Chinle, AZ
Source: Private collection (1972)
Construction: All vegetal dyed, natural white, all handspun.

Plate 23
Ganado (36" X 42")
Weaver: Unknown
Source: Courtesy, Hubbell Trading Post, Ganado, AZ (1973)
Construction: Mostly synthetic dyed, processed white, all handspun.

Plate 24
Ganado (36" X 42")
Weaver: Unknown
Source: Courtesy, Hubbell Trading Post (1973)
Construction: Mostly synthetic dyed, processed white, all handspun.

Plate 25
Ganado (36" X 42")
Weaver: Unknown
Source: Courtesy, Hubbell Trading Post, Ganado, AZ (1973)
Construction: Mostly synthetic dyed, natural carded gray, all handspun.

Plate 26
Ganado (20" X 40")
Weaver: Unknown
Source: Courtesy, Burnham Trading Post, Sanders, AZ (1987)
Construction: All commercial yarn.

Plate 27
Ganado (26" X 38")
Weaver: Bessie James
Source: Courtesy, Hubbell Trading Post, Ganado, AZ (1987)
Construction: All commercial yarn.

Plate 28
Ganado (36" X 60")
Weaver: Unknown
Source: Courtesy, Burnham Trading Post, Sanders, AZ (1987)
Construction: All commercial yarn.

Plate 29
Wide Ruins (21½" X 33½")
Weaver: Unknown
Source: Courtesy, Wide Ruins Trading Post (1973)
Construction: All vegetal dyed, natural white, all handspun.

Plate 30
Wide Ruins (24" X 36")
Weaver: Unknown
Source: Courtesy, Wide Ruins Trading Post (1973)
Construction: All vegetal dyed, natural white, all handspun.

Plate 31
Wide Ruins (28" X 36")
Weaver: Unknown
Source: Courtesy, Wide Ruins Trading Post (1973)
Construction: All vegetal dyed, natural white, all handspun.

Plate 32
Burntwater (30" X 42")
Weaver: Brenda Spencer
Source: Courtesy, Hubbell Trading Post, Ganado, AZ (1987)
Construction: All commercial yarn.

Plate 33
Burntwater (36" X 48")
Weaver: Unknown
Source: Charles & Leslie Hill collection, Lotus, CA (1982)
Construction: All vegetal dyed, all handspun.

Plate 34
Burntwater (30" X 40")
Weaver: Roselyn Begay
Source: Courtesy, Hubbell Trading Post, Ganado, AZ (1987)
Construction: All commercial yarn.

Plate 35
Burntwater (48" X 72")
Weaver: Lena Gorman
Source: Courtesy, Burnham Trading Post, Sanders, AZ (1987)
Construction: All commercial yarn.

Plate 36
Burntwater (30" X 40")
Weaver: Marvela Davis
Source: Thunderbird Lodge, Chinle, AZ (1987)
Construction: All commercial yarn.

Plate 37
Burntwater (24" X 36")
Weaver: Wanda Tracey
Source: Courtesy, Burnham Trading Post, Sanders, AZ (1987)
Construction: All commercial yarn.

Plate 38
New Lands (30" X 48")
Weaver: Laverne Yazzie
Source: Courtesy, Burnham Trading Post, Sanders, AZ (1987)
Construction: All vegetal-dyed commercial yarn.

Plate 39
New Lands (36" X 48")
Weaver: Brenda Nez
Source: Courtesy, Burnham Trading Post, Sanders, AZ (1987)
Construction: All vegetal-dyed commercial yarn.

Plate 40
Storm Pattern, Raised Outline (32" X 50")
Weaver: Rose Black Mountain, Kayenta, AZ
Source: Courtesy, Bob French Navajo Rugs, Waterflow, NM (1987)
Construction: All commercial yarn.

Plate 41
Storm Pattern, Raised Outline (32" X 58")
Weaver: Unknown
Source: Private collection (1972)
Construction: Partly synthetic dyed, natural carded gray, all handspun.

Plate 42
Storm Pattern (36" X 48")
Weaver: Unknown
Source: Courtesy, Hubbell Trading Post, Ganado, AZ (1973)
Construction: Partly synthetic dyed, natural white, natural carded gray, all handspun.

Plate 43
Storm Pattern (24" X 36")
Weaver: Unknown
Source: Courtesy, Price's All Indian Shop, Albuquerque, NM (1970)
Construction: Partly synthetic dyed, partly vegetal dyed, all handspun.

Picture Credits

Front Cover	(No. 3), National Park Service; (No. 4), Museum of New Mexico; (No. 5), National Park Service; (No. 7), Helen Hendry photo, courtesy Sallie Wagner.
Page viii	(Map), Katonah Gallery, Katonah, NY
Page 3	(Sketch), Museum of New Mexico
Page 5	Museum of New Mexico
Page 6	Smithsonian Institution
Page 7	(McNitt quote), courtesy University of Oklahoma Press; (Photo), National Park Service
Page 9	Museum of New Mexico
Page 11	(Figure), Smithsonian Institution; (Rugs), Reproduced from Hollister, 1903, courtesy Gallup, NM Public Library
Pages 12-13	Museum of New Mexico
Page 13	National Park Service
Page 14	Museum of New Mexico
Page 15	Reproduced from *The Navajo*, 1911, courtesy Gallup, NM Public Library
Page 16	National Park Service
Page 33	Gilbert Maxwell & Best-West Publications
Page 40	Museum of New Mexico
Page 45	Museum of New Mexico
Page 47	All photos reproduced from *The Navajo*, 1911, courtesy Gallup, NM Public Library
Page 48	(Both photos), Reproduced from *The Navajo*, 1911, courtesy Gallup NM Public Library
Page 58	Reproduced from *Navajo Trading Days* (Hegemann, 1963), courtesy University of New Mexico Press
Page 60	(Top), Museum of New Mexico; (Middle), National Park Service, courtesy Fred Patton, (Bottom), courtesy Sallie Wagner
Page 61	(Top), Museum of New Mexico
Page 64	Museum of New Mexico
Page 72	(Top to bottom), courtesy Sallie Wagner; Loy Tuberville photo, courtesy John Rieffer; courtesy Sallie Wagner; Loy Tuberville photo, courtesy John Rieffer; courtesy Sallie Wagner
Page 73	(All historic photos), courtesy Sallie Wagner
Page 84	Museum of New Mexico
Page 85	(Quote), *Navajo Trading Days* (Hegemann, 1963), courtesy University of New Mexico Press
Page 86	(Quote), Reproduced from *The Navajo*, 1911, courtesy Gallup NM Public Library
Page 89	(Top right), Reproduced from *Navajo Trading Days* (Hegemann, 1963), courtesy University of New Mexico Press
Page 111	(Kent Quote), courtesy *The Plateau Quarterly*, courtesy Museum of Northern Arizona

Bibliography
1882-1988

Adair, John, 1944, The Navajo and Pueblo Silversmiths: University of Oklahoma Press, Norman.

Amsden, Charles Avery, 1934, Navajo Weaving, Its Technic and its History: Fine Arts Press, Santa Barbara, California.

Bahti, Tom, 1966, Introduction To Southwestern Indian Arts and Crafts: K.C. Publications, Flagstaff, Arizona.

Bennett, Nöel, and **Bighorse, Tina,** 1971, Working with the Wool: Northland Press, Flagstaff, Arizona.

———, 1974, The Weaver's Pathway: Northland Press, Flagstaff, Arizona.

Bourke, John J., 1884, The Snake-Dance of the Moquis of Arizona: Sampson, Low, Marstan, Seale & Rivington, London, England.

Bryan, Nonabah, and **Young, Stella,** 1940, Native Navajo Dyes: U.S. Department of the Interior, Washington, D.C.

Bulow, Ernie, 1986, (Introduction), *in* The Navajo: Avanyu Publishing Company, Albuquerque, New Mexico (*Reprint*).

Burbank, E.A., 1944, Burbank Among the Indians: Caxton Printers, Caldwell, Idaho.

Coolidge, Dane, and **Coolidge, Mary,** 1930, The Navajo Indians: Houghton Mifflin Company, Boston, Massachusetts.

DeLauer, Marjel, 1975, A Century of Indian Traders and Trading Posts: *Arizona Highways Magazine,* v. 51, no. 3, Phoenix.

Dutton, Bertha, 1961, Navajo Weaving Today: Museum of New Mexico Press: Santa Fe.

Eckel, LaCharles Goodman, 1934, History of Ganado, Arizona: Museum of Northern Arizona, v. 6, no. 10, Flagstaff, Arizona.

Fontana, Bernard L., 1988, Kit Carson in Arizona: *Arizona Highways Magazine,* v. 64. no. 1, Phoenix.

Foote, Cheryl J., and **Schackel, Sandra K.,** 1986, Indian Women in New Mexico, 1535-1680, *in* New Mexico Women, Intercultural Perspectives, Joan M. Jensen and Darlis A. Miller (*eds.*): University of New Mexico Press, Albuquerque.

Getzwiler, Steve, 1984, The Fine Art of Navajo Weaving: Ray Manley Publications, Tucson, Arizona.

Gillmor, Francis, and **Wetherill, Louisa Wade,** 1952, Traders to the Navajo: University of New Mexico Press, Albuquerque.

Gilpin, Laura, 1971, The Enduring Navajo: University of Texas Press, Austin.

Granger, Byrd H. (*ed.*), 1960, Arizona Place Names: University of Arizona Press, Tucson.

Hannum, Alberta, 1944, Spin a Silver Dollar: The Story of a Desert Trading Post: The Viking Press, New York.

———, 1958, Paint the Wind: The Viking Press, New York.

Harrison, Laura Soullière, and **Spears, Beverly,** 1987, Historic Structures Report, Chinle Trading Post and Custodian's Residence, Canyon de Chelly National Monument, Arizona [*unpublished draft*]: National Park Service, Santa Fe, New Mexico.

Hegemann, Elizabeth Compton, 1963, Navaho Trading Days: University of New Mexico Press, Albuquerque.

Hill, Willard W., 1948, Navajo Trading and Trading Ritual, A Study of Cultural Dynamics: Southwestern Journal of Anthropology, v. 4, no. 4, University of New Mexico, Albuquerque.

Hollister, U.S., 1972, The Navajo and his Blanket: Rio Grande Press, Glorieta, New Mexico (*Reprint*).

Hubbell, Lorenzo, 1930, Fifty years an Indian Trader: Touring Topics, v. 22, no. 12.

Houlihan, Patrick, Collins, Jerold L., Nestor, Sarah, and Batkin, Jonathan, 1987, Harmony by Hand: McQuiston & Daughter, Inc., Dal Mar, California.

Iverson, Peter, 1988, Knowing the Land, Leaving the Land: Navajos, Hopis, and Relocation in the American West, in *Montana—The Magazine of Western History:* Montana Historical Society, v. 38, no. 1, Helena.

James, George Wharton, 1934, Indian Blankets and their Makers: A.C. McClurg & Company, Chicago, Illinois.

James, H.L., 1966, The Santa Fe Trail, *in* Guidebook of the Taos, Raton, Spanish Peaks Country: New Mexico Geological Society, Socorro.

———, 1967, The History of Fort Wingate, *in* Guidebook of the Defiance-Zuni-Mt. Taylor Region: New Mexico Geological Society, Socorro.

———, 1973, Navajo Rugs, The Regional Style, *in* Guidebook of Monument Valley and Vicinity, Arizona and Utah: New Mexico Geological Society, Socorro.

———, 1974, The Romance of Navajo Weaving: *New Mexico Magazine*, v. 52, no. 1, Santa Fe.

———, 1974, Posts and Rugs: The Story of Navajo Rugs and Their Homes: Southwest Parks and Monuments Association, Globe, Arizona.

Jeffers, Jo, 1967, Hubbell Trading Post National Historic Site: *Arizona Highways Magazine*, v. 43, no. 9, Phoenix.

Kahlenberg, Mary Hunt, and Berlant, Anthony, 1972, The Navajo Blanket: Praeger Publishing Company, Los Angeles, California.

Kaufman, Alice, and Selser, Christopher, 1985, The Navajo Weaving Tradition, 1650 to the Present: E.P. Dutton, Inc., New York.

Kent, Kate Peck, 1961, The Story of Navajo Weaving: Heard Museum, Phoenix, Arizona.

———, 1981, From Blanket to Rug: The Evolution of Navajo Weaving After 1880, in The Plateau Quarterly: Museum of Northern Arizona, v. 52, no. 4, Flagstaff.

———, 1985, Navajo Weaving: Three Centuries of Change: School of American Research Press, Santa Fe, New Mexico.

Kluckhorn, Clyde, and Leighton, Dorothea, 1962, The Navajo: Doubleday Publishing Company, Garden City, New York.

Koeing, Harriet, and Koeing, Seymour H., 1986, Navajo Weaving-Navajo Ways: Katonah Gallery, Katonah, New York.

Lesch, Alma, 1970, Vegetable Dyeing: Watson-Guptill Publishing Company: New York.

Luomala, Katherine, 1974, Navajo Weaving: Museum of New Mexico Press, El Palacio Quarterly, v. 80, no. 1, Santa Fe.

Matthews, Washington, 1882, Navajo Weavers: U.S. Bureau of American Ethnology 3rd Annual Report, Washington, D.C.

———, 1902, The Night Chant, A Navajo Ceremony: Memoirs of the American Museum of Natural History, v. 6, Washington, D.C.

———, 1968, Navajo Weavers and Silversmiths: Palmer Lake, Colorado (*Reprint*).

Maxwell, Gilbert S., 1963, Navajo Rugs—Past, Present and Future: Best-West Publications, Palm Desert, California.

McCoy, Ron, 1987, *Naalye he Bahooghan*—Where the Past is the Present: *Arizona Highways Magazine*, v. 63, no. 6, Phoenix.

McKibben, D.B., 1954, Revolt of the Navaho—1913, *in* New Mexico Historical Review: University of New Mexico Press, v. 24, no. 4, Albuquerque.

McLuhan, T.C., 1985. Dream Tracks: the Railroad and the American Indian, 1890-1930: Harry N. Abrams, Inc., New York.

McNitt, Frank, 1959, Two Gray Hills—America's Costliest Rugs: *New Mexico Magazine,* v. 37, no. 4, Santa Fe.

_____ , 1962, The Indian Traders: University of Oklahoma Press, Norman.

_____ , *(ed.),* 1964, Navajo Expedition; University of Oklahoma Press, Norman *(Reprint).*

_____ , 1972, Navajo Wars: University of New Mexico Press, Albuquerque.

Mera, H.P., 1949, Navajo Textile Arts: New Mexico Laboratory of Anthropology, Santa Fe.

Miller, Marjorie, 1972, Indian Arts and Crafts: Nash Publishing Company, Los Angeles, California.

Mills, George, 1959, Navaho Art and Culture: Taylor Museum Fine Arts Center, Colorado Springs, Colorado.

Moore, J.B., 1911, The Navajo: Williamson-Haffner Company, Denver, Colorado.

Mott, Dorothy Challis, 1931, Don Lorenzo Hubbell of Ganado: Arizona Historical Review, v. 4, no. 1, Tucson.

National Park Service, 1986, Hubbell Trading Post National Historic Site (Visitor Pamphlet): National Park Service, Washington, D.C.

Newcomb, Franc Johnson, 1964, Hosteen Klah: Navajo Medicine Man and Sand Painter: University of Oklahoma Press, Norman.

_____ , 1966, Navajo Neighbors: University of Oklahoma Press, Norman.

Pearce, T.M. *(ed.).* 1965, New Mexico Place Names: University of New Mexico Press, Albuquerque.

Pendleton, Mary, 1974, Navajo and Hopi Weaving Techniques: Collier Books, New York.

Reichard, Gladys A., 1939, Dezba: Woman of the Desert: J.J. Augustin Company, New York.

_____ , 1968, Navajo Shepherd and Weaver: Rio Grande Press, Glorieta, New Mexico *(Reprint).*

_____ , 1968, Spider Woman: Rio Grande Press, Glorieta, New Mexico (Reprint).

Richardson, Gladwell, 1986, Navajo Trader: University of Arizona Press, Tucson.

Rodee, Marian, 1981, Old Navajo Rugs: University of New Mexico Press, Albuquerque.

_____ , 1987, Weaving of the Southwest: Schiffer Publishing Company, West Chester, Pennsylvania.

Simpson, James H., 1850, Reconnaissance Expedition into the Navajo Country: U.S. Senate Document No. 64, Washington, D.C.

Spiegelberg, A.F., 1925, Navajo Blankets: Museum of New Mexico Press, El Palacio Quarterly, v. 18, nos. 10, 11, Santa Fe.

Tanner, Clara Lee, 1964, Modern Navajo Weaving: *Arizona Highways Magazine,* v. 40, no. 9, Phoenix.

_____ , 1968, Southwest Indian Craft Arts: University of Arizona Press, Tucson.

Twitchell, Ralph Emerson, 1963, The Leading Facts of New Mexico History: Horn & Wallace Publishing Company, Albuquerque, New Mexico.

Underhill, Ruth, 1944, Pueblo Crafts: Haskell Institute, Lawrence, Kansas.

_____ , 1953, Here Come the Navajo: Haskell Institute, Lawrence, Kansas.

_____ , 1956, The Navajo: University of Oklahoma Press, Norman.

U.S. Federal Trade Commission, 1973, The Trading Post System on the Navajo Reservation: U.S. Printing Office, Washington, D.C.

Utley, Robert M., 1961, The Reservation Trader in Navajo History: Museum of New Mexico Press, El Palacio Quarterly, v. 68, no. 1, Santa Fe.

Utley, Robert M., and **Washburn, Wilcomb E.,** 1977, American Heritage of the Indian Wars, *in* American Heritage, New York.

Van Valkenburgh, Richard F., 1974, A Short History of the Navajo People: Garland Publications, New York.

Watson, Editha L., 1957, Navajo Rugs: *Arizona Highways Magazine,* v. 33, no. 8, Phoenix.

———— , 1973, Navajo History: A 3,000-year Sketch, *in* Guidebook of Monument Valley and Vicinity, Arizona and Utah: New Mexico Geological Society, Socorro.

Wheat, Joe Ben, 1974, Three Centuries of Navajo Weaving: *Arizona Highways Magazine,* v. 50, no. 7, Phoenix.

————, 1981, Early Navajo Weaving, in The Plateau Quarterly, Museum of Northern Arizona, v. 52, no. 4, Flagstaff.

Whiteford, Andrew Hunter, 1970, North American Indian Arts, Western Publishing Company, New York.

. . . .

Pertinent titles issued by the Laboratory of Anthropology (Technological Series), Santa Fe, New Mexico.

(1) Bulletin No. 3—Navajo Blankets of the Classic Period (1938)

(2) Bulletin No. 5—The Slave Blanket (1938)

(3) Bulletin No. 6—Pictorial Blankets (1938)

(4) Bulletin No. 9—Wedge Weave Blankets (1939)

(5) Bulletin No. 12—The Zoning Treatment in Navajo Blanket Design (1940)

(6) Bulletin No. 13—The Chinlee Rug (1942)

(7) Bulletin No. 14—Navajo Twilled Weaving (1943)

(8) Bulletin No. 15—Navajo Woven Dresses (1943)

(9) Bulletin No. 16—Cloth Strip Blankets of the Navajo (1945)

Index